Time Mastery

A Practical Guide for Muslims to
Maximise Time & Productivity
for a Life Filled With Barakah

SARAH GULFRAZ

Copyright © 2024 Sarah Gulfraz

Sarah Gulfraz has asserted her right to be identified as the author of this Work in accordance with the Copyright, Designs and Patents Act 1988.

All rights reserved.

No portion of this book may be reproduced in any form, stored in a retrieval system, stored in a database, or published/transmitted in any form or by any means, electronic, mechanical, photocopying, recording or otherwise, without prior written permission of the publisher.

Dedication

~ **Bismillah** ~

May Allah (swt) accept our efforts and grant us success in this life and the next. Ameen.

In dedication to my loving family and all their support.

Contents

1. Understanding Time in Islam — 1
2. Principles of Islamic Time Management — 16
3. Setting Priorities and Goals — 34
4. Planning and Organisation — 47
5. Time Management Tools and Resources — 61
6. Dealing with Time Wasters — 75
7. Balancing Work, Worship, and Rest — 87
8. Overcoming Procrastination and Laziness — 101
9. Delegation and Collaboration — 115
10. Stress Management and Resilience — 127
11. Time Management in Ramadan and Other Special Occasions — 144
12. Continuous Improvement and Self-Reflection — 162
13. Barakah and Blessings in Time Management — 179
14. Achieving Spiritual Fulfilment Through Effective Time Management — 187

Find Out More — 193

Chapter One

Understanding Time in Islam

Imagine a treasure so precious that every moment you waste it is like throwing gold into the wind. In Islam, time is considered such a treasure. It's a resource that Allah has given to us in limited measure, and it's our duty to use it wisely. Whether we're spending our time in prayer, work, or with our loved ones, every second counts.

The Prophet Muhammad (peace be upon him) also highlighted the importance of time. He said,

> *"Take advantage of five before five: your youth before old age, your health before sickness, your wealth before poverty, your free time before becoming busy, and your life before death" (Sahih Bukhari)*

This profound hadith encapsulates the transient nature of life and the fleeting opportunities we have. Each aspect mentioned—youth, health, wealth, free time, and life—is a temporary blessing that can be lost at any moment. The Prophet (peace be upon him) urges us to seize these moments and use them for good, whether that's in worship, self-improvement, helping others, or fulfilling our responsibilities.

In Islam, managing time effectively isn't just about being productive in a worldly sense; it's also about seeking Barakah, or divine blessings, in everything we do.

Barakah isn't just about having more time; it's about having the right quality of time that allows us to achieve more with less effort. This concept is beautifully intertwined with our daily routines and activities.

Think about starting your day with the Fajr prayer. This early morning practice not only sets a peaceful tone for the day but also brings immense Barakah. It's a way to seek Allah's blessings from the very beginning of the day.

Similarly, incorporating Quran recitation and Dhikr (remembrance of Allah) throughout the day can transform ordinary moments into spiritually enriching experiences.

Effective time management in Islam is about striking a balance. It's about giving due attention to our religious obligations, personal responsibilities, and professional duties. When we prioritise correctly and manage our time well, we invite Barakah into our lives.

This doesn't just make us more productive; it also brings a sense of fulfilment and peace that comes from knowing we're living our lives in accordance with our faith.

The role of time management in achieving personal and spiritual growth cannot be overstated. It's through disciplined time management that we can carve out moments for self-reflection, prayer, and connecting with Allah.

This not only helps in our personal development but also ensures that our spiritual well-being is nurtured.

Understanding the Importance of Time in Islamic Perspective

Quranic verses emphasising the value of time and its significance in life

Time is a precious and finite resource, a concept that Islam profoundly addresses through the Quran. Allah repeatedly emphasise the importance of time, urging believers to reflect on its passage and make the most of it. One of the most striking verses on the significance of time is from Surah Al-Asr:

> *"By time, indeed, mankind is in loss, except for those who have believed and done righteous deeds and advised each other to truth and advised each other to patience"* - *Quran (103:1-3)*

This short surah encapsulates the essence of Islamic time management. The reference to "time" (Al-Asr) underscores the fleeting nature of our existence. Scholars like Ibn Kathir and Al-Qurtubi explain that Allah swears by time to highlight its supreme importance. The surah warns that without faith, good deeds, truth, and patience, humans are at a profound loss. It serves as a reminder that time must be filled with meaningful actions aligned with faith and righteousness.

Another profound verse is found in Surah Al-Mu'minun:

> *"Then We made the sperm-drop into a clinging clot, and We made the clot into a lump (of flesh), and We made (from) the lump, bones, and We covered the bones with*

flesh; then We developed him into another creation. So blessed is Allah, the best of creators" - Quran (23:14)

This verse, while describing the stages of human creation, subtly points to the process and passage of time in our lives. It emphasises that every stage of our existence is meticulously planned by Allah, reminding us to value and respect the time we are given.

In Surah Yunus, Allah says,

"It is He who made the sun a shining light and the moon a derived light and determined for it phases - that you may know the number of years and account (of time). Allah has not created this except in truth. He details the signs for a people who know" - Quran (10:5)

This verse highlights the cosmic order and the precise measurement of time. Tafsir scholars like Al-Jalalayn explain that the mention of the sun and moon's phases is a call to reflect on the natural phenomena that govern time. It urges believers to use these signs to measure their days and years, encouraging a conscious awareness of the passage of time.

Reflecting on Surah Al-Insan, Allah says:

"Has there (not) come upon man a period of time when he was not a thing (even) mentioned?" - Quran (76:1)

This verse is a profound reminder of the temporality of human existence. Tafsir Ibn Kathir notes that this verse prompts humans to recognise their humble beginnings and the transient nature of their lives. It serves to remind us that our time on earth is limited and must be used wisely.

Surah Al-An'am also speaks to the value of time:

> *"And it is He who made the night and day in succession for whoever desires to remember or desires gratitude"* - Quran (25:62)

This verse, according to scholars like As-Sa'di, emphasises the alternation of day and night as a blessing from Allah. It invites believers to use these cycles as opportunities for remembrance and gratitude, reinforcing the importance of time in daily life.

Quran repeatedly draws our attention to the passage of time and its significance. These verses and their tafseer highlight that time is a trust from Allah, one that we must use to fulfil our spiritual and worldly obligations. By appreciating the value of time, we align our lives with the divine wisdom and strive towards achieving success in both this life and the hereafter.

Prophetic sayings (Hadiths) highlighting the importance of utilising time wisely

The teachings of Prophet Muhammad (peace be upon him) are filled with wisdom on the value and utilisation of time. Through his sayings and actions, he provided clear guidance on making the most of our time, emphasising the importance of balancing our worldly responsibilities with our spiritual obligations.

One of the most famous hadiths on this topic is:

> *"The feet of the son of Adam shall not move from before his Lord on the Day of Judgment until he is asked about five things: about his life and how he spent it, his youth and how he used it, his wealth and how he earned it and*

spent it, and what he did with what he knew" (Sunan At-Tirmidhi)

This hadith underscores that time, particularly the periods of youth and life, is a trust for which we will be held accountable. The Prophet (peace be upon him) highlights that our actions and how we manage our time will be scrutinised, reminding us to live our lives with purpose and responsibility.

The Prophet Muhammad (peace be upon him) also said:

"There are two blessings which many people waste: health and free time" (Sahih Bukhari)

This hadith points out that people often take their health and leisure for granted, failing to use them in ways that benefit their spiritual and worldly lives. It serves as a warning to not let these blessings go to waste but to use them wisely while we have them.

Another hadith that emphasises the use of time is:

"Seize the opportunity before five things come to you: your old age, your sickness, your poverty, your death, and the Dajjal (Antichrist)" (Ibn Majah)

This saying teaches us to live in the present and make the most of each day, reflecting the uncertainty of life and the importance of not procrastinating.

These hadiths, filled with profound insights, guide us on how to use our time wisely. The Prophet (peace be upon him) emphasised the value of time through both his words and his exemplary lifestyle, offering timeless advice that helps us lead balanced, purposeful, and fulfilling lives. By following these teachings, we can ensure that our time is spent in ways that are pleasing to Allah and beneficial to our overall well-being.

Link Between Time Management and Productivity in Islam

Concept of Barakah (blessings) and its relation to effective time utilisation

In Islam, time is a treasure bestowed upon us by Allah, and how we utilise it can profoundly impact our productivity and spiritual growth. Central to this concept is Barakah, the divine blessings that enhance the quality and outcome of our actions.

Barakah isn't just about having more time; it's about making the most of the time we have. When we align our activities with Islamic principles and seek Allah's guidance, our efforts become more fruitful, and we achieve more with less.

The Quran reminds us of the importance of righteousness in attracting Barakah. Allah says:

> *"And whatever you spend in good – it will be fully repaid to you, and you will not be wronged."* - Quran (2:272)

This verse emphasises that living a life of faith and piety invites divine blessings into our time and endeavours.

The Prophet Muhammad (peace be upon him) exemplified effective time management through his daily routines and teachings. He emphasised the significance of starting the day with Fajr prayer, saying:

> *"O Allah, bless my nation in their early mornings"*
> *(Sunan Ibn Majah)*

By beginning our day with worship and remembrance of Allah, we set a positive tone and invite Barakah into our time.

Intention (niyyah) is another key aspect of attracting Barakah. When we purify our intentions and dedicate our time to activities that align with seeking Allah's pleasure, even the simplest tasks become acts of worship.

Prioritizing tasks is essential for effective time management. By focusing on beneficial activities and seeking Allah's assistance, we can ensure that our time is spent wisely and productively.

Gratitude and contentment also play a crucial role in attracting Barakah. The Prophet (peace be upon him) said:

> *"Whoever is not grateful for small things will not be grateful for large things"* *(Musnad Ahmad)*

When we recognise and appreciate the blessings in our lives, including our time, we attract more divine blessings.

How to seek blessings in daily activities?

In the hustle and bustle of daily life, it's easy to overlook the opportunities for blessings that surround us. Yet, in Islam, every moment presents a chance to invite divine favour into our lives. Here are some practical ways to seek blessings in our daily activities:

Begin with Bismillah

Start every task with the name of Allah. Whether it's something as simple as cooking a meal or embarking on a new project, invoking the name of Allah at the outset sets the stage for blessings to flow.

Perform Tasks with Excellence

The Prophet Muhammad (peace be upon him) said:

> *"Allah loves, when one of you does something, that he does it in the most excellent manner" (Sahih Muslim)*

By striving for excellence in everything we do, whether it's our work, studies, or interactions with others, we open ourselves up to receiving Allah's blessings.

Remember Allah Frequently

Incorporate Dhikr (remembrance of Allah) into your daily routine. Whether it's reciting SubhanAllah (glory be to Allah), Alhamdulillah (praise be to Allah), or Allahu Akbar (Allah is the greatest), frequent remembrance of Allah keeps us connected to Him and invites blessings into our lives.

Give in Charity

The Prophet (peace be upon him) said:

> *"Charity does not decrease wealth" (Sahih Muslim)*

By giving generously, we not only help those in need but also purify our wealth and attract blessings from Allah.

Seek Knowledge

The pursuit of knowledge is highly encouraged in Islam. The Prophet (peace be upon him) said:

> *"Whoever takes a path upon which to obtain knowledge, Allah makes the path to Paradise easy for him." (Sahih Muslim)*

By seeking knowledge and acting upon it, we open ourselves up to receiving blessings from Allah.

Be Kind and Compassionate

The Prophet Muhammad (peace be upon him) said:

> *"The merciful will be shown mercy by the Most Merciful. Be merciful to those on the earth and the One in the heavens will have mercy upon you" (Sunan At-Tirmidhi)*

By showing kindness and compassion to others, we emulate the traits of Allah and invite His blessings into our lives.

Make Dua (Supplication)

Never underestimate the power of dua. The Prophet (peace be upon him) said:

> *"Nothing can change the Divine decree except dua"*
> *(Sunan At-Tirmidhi)*

Take time each day to make heartfelt supplications to Allah, asking for His blessings in all aspects of your life.

Practice Patience and Gratitude

The Prophet (peace be upon him) said:

> *"Amazing is the affair of the believer, verily all of his affair is good and this is not for anyone except the believer. If something of good/happiness befalls him he is grateful and that is good for him. If something of harm befalls him he is patient and that is good for him" (Sahih Muslim)*

By cultivating patience and gratitude, we demonstrate our trust in Allah's wisdom and invite His blessings into our lives.

Conclude with Alhamdulillah

At the end of each day, take a moment to reflect on the blessings you've received and express gratitude to Allah by saying Alhamdulillah (praise be to Allah). Recognizing and acknowledging Allah's blessings in our lives is itself a source of immense blessings.

Role of time management in achieving personal and spiritual growth

When we talk about personal and spiritual growth, time management isn't just a nice-to-have skill; it's essential. In Islam, time is a gift from

Allah, and managing it well is a form of worship. Let's explore how effective time management can help us grow both personally and spiritually.

Balancing Deen and Dunya

In Islam, there's a strong emphasis on balancing our worldly life (Dunya) with our religious duties (Deen). Allah says in the Quran:

> *"But seek, with what Allah has given you, the home of the Hereafter; and [yet], do not forget your share of the world"* - Quran (28:77)

This verse highlights the importance of not neglecting our worldly responsibilities while striving for spiritual success. Effective time management allows us to balance our work, family life, and spiritual obligations without compromising any aspect.

Prioritising Your Spiritual Goals

To grow spiritually, we need to prioritise our spiritual goals. This means setting aside time for prayer, Quran recitation, and Dhikr (remembrance of Allah). The Prophet Muhammad (peace be upon him) emphasised the importance of daily worship, saying:

> *"Whoever prays Fajr in congregation, then sits remembering Allah until the sun rises, then prays two Rak'ahs, will have a reward like that of Hajj and Umrah." (Tirmidhi)*

By allocating specific times for these activities, we ensure that our spiritual practices become a consistent part of our daily routine.

Seeking Barakah in Time

Barakah, or divine blessing, can make a significant difference in how we experience and utilise our time. The Quran states:

> *"And if only the people of the cities had believed and feared Allah, We would have opened upon them blessings from the heaven and the earth"* - Quran (7:96)

By living righteously and seeking Allah's pleasure, we invite Barakah into our lives, making our efforts more fruitful and our time more productive.

Self-Reflection and Accountability

Self-reflection is a key component of personal growth. The Prophet Muhammad (peace be upon him) advised:

> *"Take account of yourselves before you are taken to account"* (Sunan Tirmidhi)

By regularly assessing our actions and how we spend our time, we can identify areas for improvement and make necessary adjustments. This habit of self-reflection helps us stay aligned with our spiritual goals and personal aspirations.

Maximizing Productivity

Time management isn't just about being busy; it's about being productive. The Prophet (peace be upon him) said:

> *"The strong believer is better and more beloved to Allah than the weak believer, while there is good in both. Strive for that which will benefit you, seek the help of Allah, and do not feel helpless" (Sahih Muslim)*

By focusing on beneficial activities and seeking Allah's help, we can ensure that our time is spent wisely and productively.

Creating a Balanced Routine

A balanced routine that includes time for worship, work, family, and rest is crucial for overall well-being. The Prophet Muhammad (peace be upon him) led by example, maintaining a well-organised daily schedule that included time for all important activities.

By following his example, we can create a balanced routine that caters to all aspects of our lives.

Personal Development

Effective time management also contributes to personal development. By setting clear goals and managing our time well, we can pursue knowledge, develop new skills, and achieve our personal aspirations. The Quran encourages us to seek knowledge and grow:

> *"Say, 'Are those who know equal to those who do not know?'" - Quran (39:9)*

Allocating time for personal development activities ensures continuous growth and improvement.

Strengthening Family Bonds

Time management helps us allocate quality time for our families. The Prophet Muhammad (peace be upon him) placed great emphasis on maintaining strong family ties, saying:

> *"The best of you are those who are best to their families, and I am the best among you to my family" (Sunan Ibn Majah)*

By managing our time effectively, we can strengthen our relationships and fulfil our responsibilities towards our loved ones.

Chapter Two

Principles of Islamic Time Management

Life can be overwhelming with endless tasks and responsibilities. Prioritisation helps us navigate through this chaos by focusing on what truly matters. Islam provides a clear framework for identifying our priorities based on the teachings of the Quran and the Hadith. The Quran guides us in setting our priorities straight. Allah says:

> *"O you who have believed, bow and prostrate and worship your Lord and do good - that you may succeed." - Quran (22:77)*

This verse emphasises the importance of worship and doing good, highlighting that fulfilling our religious obligations should always come first. Once we've taken care of our spiritual duties, we can then allocate time for personal and professional responsibilities. A balanced life is one where both religious obligations and personal responsibilities are met. The Prophet Muhammad (peace be upon him) led a life where he gave due time to worship, family, and community. By following his example, we can allocate our time effectively, ensuring that every aspect of our life receives the attention it deserves.

Consistency is the secret sauce of successful time management. It's not enough to have a great plan; you need the discipline to stick to it every day.

Daily routines help us build momentum and create a sense of stability. By maintaining consistent habits, such as regular prayer times, Quran recitation, and productive work hours, we cultivate a disciplined lifestyle that enhances both our personal and spiritual growth.

Tawakkul (Reliance on Allah) and Planning

Balancing between reliance on Allah and taking proactive steps

Tawakkul, or reliance on Allah, is a cornerstone of Islamic faith. It's the deep-seated trust in Allah's wisdom and plan for us, recognising that He is the ultimate provider and planner. But how does this concept fit with the idea of planning and taking proactive steps in our daily lives? Islam beautifully balances Tawakkul with proactive efforts, teaching us that while we trust Allah, we must also strive and work diligently.

The concept of Tawakkul is eloquently explained in the Quran:

> *"And put your trust in Allah, and sufficient is Allah as a disposer of affairs"* - Quran (33:3)

This verse highlights that while we should rely on Allah in all matters, we also have a role to play. This is further emphasised in the hadith where the Prophet Muhammad (peace be upon him) said,

> *"Tie your camel first, and then put your trust in Allah"* *(Sunan At-Tirmidhi)*

This hadith beautifully illustrates the balance between taking necessary precautions and having faith in Allah.

The Harmony of Tawakkul and Planning

Planning is an essential aspect of effective time management and productivity. It involves setting clear goals, outlining steps to achieve them, and taking action. However, in Islam, planning goes hand in hand with Tawakkul. We plan with the understanding that success ultimately comes from Allah. This dual approach ensures that we are not overwhelmed by the outcomes of our efforts because we trust in Allah's wisdom.

Imagine a farmer who wants to grow crops. He needs to prepare the land, plant the seeds, water them, and take care of the plants. This is his proactive effort. However, he also knows that the growth of his crops depends on factors beyond his control, like the weather. Here, his Tawakkul comes into play. He trusts that Allah will take care of what he cannot control. Similarly, in our lives, we must make our best efforts while trusting Allah with the results.

Setting Goals Aligned with Islamic Values

In planning, it's crucial to set goals that align with Islamic values. Our goals should not only aim for personal success but also for spiritual growth and benefit to the community. The Quran advises:

> *"So be patient. Indeed, the promise of Allah is truth. And let them not disquiet you who are not certain [in faith]"*
> *- Quran (30:60)*

Patience and perseverance are essential in goal-setting, trusting that Allah's promise holds true for those who strive with sincerity.

For instance, when setting career goals, we should ensure that our work is Halal (permissible) and beneficial to society. When planning our daily routines, we should prioritise our prayers and spiritual activities, knowing that these actions bring Barakah (blessings) into our lives. The Prophet Muhammad (peace be upon him) said:

> *"Whoever is mindful of Allah, He will make a way out for him and provide for him from sources he never could imagine"* - Quran (65:2-3)

This hadith encourages us to maintain our faith while working towards our goals.

Balancing Effort and Trust

Balancing effort and trust in Allah is a dynamic process. It involves continuous self-reflection and adjustment. The Quran says:

> *"And those who strive for Us - We will surely guide them to Our ways. And indeed, Allah is with the doers of good"* - Quran (29:69)

This verse assures us that Allah supports those who put in the effort while maintaining their faith in Him.

In practice, this balance can be achieved by starting every task with Bismillah (in the name of Allah), making sincere Dua (prayer) for guidance and success, and then diligently working towards our goals.

At the end of the day, we should reflect on our efforts, seeking forgiveness for shortcomings and thanking Allah for any achievements.

Setting goals aligned with Islamic values

Every action in Islam begins with a clear intention (Niyyah). The Prophet Muhammad (peace be upon him) said:

> *"Actions are judged by intentions, and everyone will be rewarded according to their intentions" (Sahih Bukhari)*

This hadith emphasises the importance of having pure intentions when setting goals. Before we embark on any task, it's crucial to ask ourselves why we are doing it and ensure our intentions are aligned with seeking Allah's pleasure.

For example, if you're setting a career goal, reflect on how this career can help you serve your community and fulfil your religious duties. By setting goals with the intention of pleasing Allah, we invite Barakah (blessings) into our efforts, making them more meaningful and successful.

Prioritising Spiritual Goals

In Islam, our primary focus should always be on our relationship with Allah. Therefore, setting spiritual goals is of utmost importance. These goals can include regular prayer (Salat), Quran recitation, learning Islamic knowledge, and engaging in acts of charity. Allah says in the Quran:

> *"So remember Me; I will remember you. And be grateful to Me and do not deny Me." - Quran (2:152)*

This verse emphasises the importance of remembering and worshiping Allah, which should be at the core of our spiritual goals.

A practical approach to setting spiritual goals is to incorporate them into your daily routine. For instance, aim to pray all five daily prayers on time, read a few verses of the Quran every day, and make time for Dhikr (remembrance of Allah). These small, consistent actions can lead to significant spiritual growth over time.

Balancing Worldly and Spiritual Aspirations

Islam teaches us to seek a balance between our worldly and spiritual lives. Allah says:

> *"And We have certainly made for you on the earth an abode, and made for you therein [ways of] livelihood. Little are you grateful."* - Quran (7:10)

This verse encourages us to appreciate the provisions given by Allah while keeping our focus on the Hereafter. Balancing these two aspects ensures that our efforts in this world contribute to our success in the Hereafter.

When setting worldly goals, such as advancing in your career or acquiring new skills, consider how these goals can benefit your spiritual life and the community. For example, if you aim to become a doctor, your intention could be to help those in need, a highly valued act in Islam. The Prophet Muhammad (peace be upon him) said:

> *"The best of people are those that bring most benefit to the rest of mankind" (Daraqutni)*

This hadith highlights the importance of setting goals that contribute positively to society.

Seeking Knowledge

One of the most rewarding goals in Islam is seeking knowledge. Setting goals to acquire both religious and worldly knowledge can enhance our understanding and practice of Islam. Whether it's learning more about the Quran and Hadith or pursuing higher education in your field, these goals should be aimed at personal growth and community benefit.

Reflecting and Adjusting Goals

Regular reflection is key to ensuring our goals remain aligned with Islamic values. The Quran encourages self-reflection:

> *"Then why do you not reflect if you are not to be recompensed?" - Quran (56:62)*

Take time to assess your progress, reflect on your intentions, and make necessary adjustments to stay on the right path. This continuous process of evaluation helps keep our goals relevant and aligned with our faith.

Setting goals aligned with Islamic values involves a harmonious blend of intention, prioritisation of spiritual goals, balance between worldly and spiritual aspirations, seeking knowledge, and regular reflection.

This alignment brings Barakah into our lives, helping us achieve success in both this world and the Hereafter. Through sincere intentions and diligent efforts, we can fulfil our duties as Muslims while striving for personal and spiritual excellence.

Prioritisation in Islam

Identifying priorities based on Quranic teachings

Prioritisation is about determining what matters most and focusing our efforts on those areas. In Islam, this involves recognising our obligations towards Allah, our responsibilities towards others, and our duties to ourselves. The Quran provides profound guidance on how to prioritise our lives effectively.

Worship as the Primary Priority

The foremost priority in a Muslim's life is worshiping Allah. The Quran emphasises this fundamental duty:

> *"And I did not create the jinn and mankind except to worship Me"* - *Quran (51:56)*

This verse underscores that our ultimate purpose is to worship Allah, making our religious obligations the highest priority.

Prayer (Salat) is a critical aspect of worship. Allah commands in the Quran:

> *"Indeed, prayer has been decreed upon the believers a decree of specified times"* - *Quran (4:103)*

Fulfilling our daily prayers on time should be non-negotiable, as it is the primary means of maintaining our connection with Allah. By prioritising Salat, we ensure that our spiritual well-being is nurtured, which in turn positively influences all other aspects of our lives.

Family and Community Responsibilities

After fulfilling our obligations to Allah, our next priority is our responsibilities towards our family and community. The Quran emphasises the importance of maintaining strong family ties and being kind to others. Allah says:

> *"And We have enjoined upon man [care] for his parents. His mother carried him, [increasing her] in weakness upon weakness, and his weaning is in two years. Be grateful to Me and to your parents; to Me is the [final] destination"* - Quran (31:14)

This verse highlights the importance of honouring and caring for our parents, which is a fundamental priority in Islam.

Moreover, the Prophet Muhammad (peace be upon him) said:

> *"The best of you are those who are best to their families"* (Sunan Ibn Majah)

This hadith reinforces the idea that our behaviour towards our family members is a significant indicator of our faith. Prioritising family responsibilities ensures that we fulfil our duties as Muslims and contribute to a harmonious and supportive home environment.

Personal Development and Self-Care

While our obligations to Allah and our family are paramount, Islam also encourages us to prioritise our personal development and self-care. The Quran states:

> "O you who have believed, protect yourselves and your families from a Fire whose fuel is people and stones." - Quran (66:6)

This verse reminds us that while striving for the Hereafter, we should also take care of our worldly needs and well-being, ensuring we are in a good state to fulfil our religious and familial obligations.

Personal development can include seeking knowledge, improving skills, and maintaining physical and mental health. The Prophet Muhammad (peace be upon him) said:

> "Be keen on that which benefits you and seek help in Allah and do not give up." (Sahih Muslim)

This hadith encourages us to strive for strength and excellence in all aspects of our lives, including our physical and intellectual capabilities.

Balancing Worldly Duties and Spiritual Growth

This balance ensures that we do not neglect our responsibilities in either realm.

To achieve this balance, we must prioritise activities that enhance both our worldly success and spiritual well-being. For example, pursuing a career that benefits society and allows us to fulfil our financial obligations can be a way of serving Allah and His creation.

Allocating time to fulfil religious obligations and personal responsibilities

Balancing religious obligations and personal responsibilities is essential for a harmonious life. In Islam, time is viewed as a trust from Allah, and we must use it wisely to fulfil our duties.

Start with Prayer (Salat)

The cornerstone of a Muslim's daily schedule is the five daily prayers. The Quran emphasises:

> *"O you who have believed, be persistently standing in prayer, bowing and prostrating, and seeking the favor of Allah - that you may be successful." (Quran 2:238)*

Establishing fixed times for prayer creates a framework for our day, ensuring our spiritual obligations are met consistently.

Integrate Spiritual Practices

In addition to Salat, incorporate Quran recitation, Dhikr (remembrance of Allah), and Dua (supplication) into your daily routine. These practices provide spiritual nourishment and keep our connection with Allah strong. Allocating specific times for these activities helps integrate them seamlessly into our day.

Prioritise Family and Social Responsibilities

After fulfilling our obligations to Allah, prioritise time for family and community.

Allocate time for family meals, conversations, and shared activities to strengthen bonds.

Balance Work and Personal Development

Islam encourages personal development and fulfilling professional responsibilities. Allocate time for work, ensuring that it aligns with ethical principles and benefits society. Additionally, set aside time for learning and personal growth.

Plan and Reflect

Use planning tools like to-do lists or schedules to organise your day. Reflect on your daily activities to ensure they align with your priorities. The Quran advises:

> *"And We have made the night and day two signs, and We erased the sign of the night and made the sign of the day visible that you may seek bounty from your Lord and may know the number of years and the account [of time]. And everything We have set out in detail."* - Quran (17:12)

Regular reflection helps maintain focus and balance.

Discipline and Consistency

Importance of consistency in daily routines

You know how they say, "Slow and steady wins the race"? That's pretty much the essence of consistency, especially when it comes to our daily routines. In Islam, consistency isn't about rigid schedules or being perfect all the time. It's about making regular, small efforts that add up to big results over time. The Prophet Muhammad (peace be upon him) put it perfectly:

> *"The most beloved deed to Allah is the most regular and constant, even if it were little" (Sahih Bukhari)*

Let's break down why sticking to our routines is so important.

Keep Your Worship on Point

First things first, let's talk about prayer (Salat). Those five daily prayers are like the anchors of our day. The Quran says:

> *"Establish prayer at the decline of the sun [sunset] and at the rising of the sun [sunrise] and [at other times] during the day and night. And fear not [the reproach of people] – for to Allah is [all] worship [and] to Him [alone] is sincere devotion." (Quran 11:116)*

Making sure we pray at the right times every day helps keep our connection with Allah strong. It's like having five mini-meditation sessions spread throughout the day, giving us regular check-ins with our faith.

Build Your Spiritual Habits

Besides prayer, there are other spiritual practices that can become part of our daily routine. Reading a bit of the Quran, doing Dhikr (remembrance of Allah), and making Dua (supplication) are all great ways to keep our spiritual life vibrant. Think of these practices as daily vitamins for the soul. The Prophet Muhammad (peace be upon him) said:

> *"Whoever is consistent in reciting the Quran will be protected from error" (Sunan Ibn Majah)*

So, a little bit every day goes a long way.

Boost Your Productivity

Consistency isn't just about spirituality; it's a game-changer for your personal and work life too. Setting specific times for tasks and sticking to them can make you way more efficient. It's like having a personal trainer for your time. You avoid procrastination and get things done. The Quran gives us a nudge in this direction:

> *"So be patient. Indeed, the promise of Allah is truth. And ask forgiveness for your sin and exalt [Allah] with praise of your Lord in the evening and the morning." - Quran (40:55)*

Basically, if you put in the effort regularly, you'll see the results.

Stay Healthy

Let's not forget about taking care of our bodies. Regular exercise, eating right, and getting enough sleep are all parts of a balanced routine. The Prophet Muhammad (peace be upon him) said:

> *"Your body has a right over you" (Sahih Bukhari)*

So, think of those workouts and healthy meals as acts of worship. By sticking to these healthy habits, you'll have more energy to do everything else.

Handle Life's Curveballs

Life can be unpredictable, and that's where consistency really helps. When you have solid routines, you've got something steady to hold onto when things get chaotic. The Quran reassures us:

> *"Verily, with hardship comes ease"* - Quran (94:6)

Keeping up with your routines during tough times can give you a sense of normalcy and control.

Be a Role Model

When you're consistent, you're not just helping yourself; you're setting a great example for others. Kids, especially, learn by watching. If they see you praying regularly, reading the Quran, and managing your time well, they're likely to pick up those habits too. The Prophet Muhammad (peace be upon him) said:

> *"The best of you are those who learn the Quran and teach it"* (Sahih Bukhari)

Your actions can inspire others to follow suit.

Cultivating self-discipline through Islamic principles

Everything in Islam begins with intentions. When you set out to build self-discipline, start by setting a clear, sincere intention. Ask yourself why you want to be more disciplined. Maybe it's to be more consistent in your prayers, to get healthier, or to be more productive at work. Whatever it is, make sure your intention is to seek Allah's pleasure.

Embrace Prayer as a Discipline Anchor

One of the best ways to build self-discipline is through regular prayer (Salat). The five daily prayers are not just acts of worship; they are also excellent practice in maintaining a routine. The Quran says:

> *"Be patient in your prayers and in whatever disaster befalls you. Indeed, this is of the obligation upon the believers." (Quran 2:153)*

By committing to these consistent prayers throughout life's challenges, you train yourself in discipline. It's a daily reminder to pause, reflect, and reconnect with Allah, which can provide stability and focus in other areas of your life.

Practice Fasting

Fasting, especially during Ramadan, is a powerful exercise in self-discipline. The Quran says:

> *"O you who have believed, decreed upon you is fasting as it was decreed upon those before you that you may become righteous"* - *Quran (2:183)*

Fasting teaches you to control your physical desires and impulses, which strengthens your overall self-control. It's not just about abstaining from food and drink; it's about being mindful of your actions, thoughts, and intentions throughout the day.

Prioritise Knowledge and Learning

Islam places a high value on seeking knowledge. The Prophet Muhammad (peace be upon him) said:

> *"Seek knowledge from the cradle to the grave." (Al-Bayhaqi)*

Make learning a part of your daily routine, whether it's religious knowledge or skills for personal and professional growth. Setting aside time each day for study requires discipline and can significantly enrich your life.

This habit can also inspire a more disciplined approach to other areas of your life.

Use the Power of Dua

Dua (supplication) is a powerful tool in Islam. When striving for self-discipline, don't forget to ask Allah for help. The Prophet Muhammad (peace be upon him) taught us to make Dua for everything, big or small.

A heartfelt Dua can provide the strength and resolve you need to stay disciplined. The Quran reassures us:

> *"And your Lord says, 'Call upon Me; I will respond to you'" - Quran (40:60)*

Regularly turning to Allah for guidance and support can help reinforce your efforts.

Establish a Routine

Creating and sticking to a daily routine can significantly enhance your self-discipline. Start with small, manageable changes, like waking up early for Fajr prayer, scheduling time for Quran recitation, or setting specific times for work and relaxation.

Consistency in small actions builds a foundation for greater discipline.

Accountability and Reflection

Holding yourself accountable is crucial for self-discipline. At the end of each day, reflect on your actions and evaluate how well you've stuck to your goals. The Quran advises:

> *"Indeed, Allah will not change the condition of a people until they change what is in themselves." - Quran (13:11)*

Regular self-reflection helps you stay on track and make necessary adjustments.

Seek Support from Community

Islam encourages community and mutual support. Surround yourself with people who inspire you and share your values. Join study circles, attend mosque activities, or engage in community service. Being part of a supportive community can motivate you to maintain discipline and stay committed to your goals.

Chapter Three

Setting Priorities and Goals

Think about what truly matters to you, both personally and professionally. Reflecting on your values, responsibilities, and aspirations can help you set clear priorities. In Islam, this is guided by Maqasid al-Shariah, which focuses on preserving faith, life, intellect, family, and wealth. Aligning your goals with these principles ensures that your efforts are not just beneficial to you but also pleasing to Allah.

When it comes to setting goals, being specific and strategic is key. The SMART approach—Specific, Measurable, Achievable, Relevant, Time-bound—can help you create clear and actionable plans. This method keeps you focused, allows you to track your progress, and makes it easier to adjust your plans as needed.

But there's more to goal-setting than just being organised. In Islam, making Dua (supplication) and relying on Allah (Tawakkul) are essential parts of the process. The Prophet Muhammad (peace be upon him) said:

"Dua is the essence of worship" (Tirmidhi)

This means that while you plan and work hard, you should also ask for Allah's guidance and support. It's about recognising that success ultimately comes from Him.

Relying on Allah doesn't mean sitting back and doing nothing. It means putting in your best effort and then trusting Allah with the outcome. Prophet Muhammad (peace be upon him) said:

"Tie your camel and then trust in Allah" (At-Tirmidhi)

This combination of effort and trust brings blessings into your endeavours and provides peace, knowing that Allah is with you every step of the way.

In this chapter, we'll explore how to set priorities and goals that align with your Islamic values. We'll cover practical strategies for effective goal setting and show you how to integrate Islamic principles into your planning process.

Identifying Personal and Professional Priorities

Defining short-term and long-term goals based on Islamic values

Life can be a whirlwind of responsibilities, aspirations, and endless to-do lists. So, how do you figure out what's really important?

Let's break it down and see how you can identify your personal and professional priorities, setting both short-term and long-term goals that align with your Islamic values.

Understanding What Matters Most

First off, it's essential to take a step back and think about what truly matters to you. This means reflecting on your values, responsibilities, and the things that bring you joy and fulfilment. Islam gives us a great framework for this through the concept of Maqasid al-Shariah, preserving faith, life, intellect, family, and wealth. These objectives help us align our goals with what's important in both our worldly and spiritual lives.

Personal Priorities

Start by looking at your personal life. What are the things you value most? Is it spending time with family, improving your health, or perhaps gaining more knowledge about Islam? Personal priorities often revolve around our immediate environment and relationships. Islam places a strong emphasis on family, community, and self-improvement.

Think about setting goals that reflect these values. For example, you might aim to spend more quality time with your family, learn something new each day, or improve your physical health through regular exercise and a balanced diet. These are all personal priorities that align with Islamic teachings.

Professional Priorities

Next, let's look at your professional life. Your career is not just about earning a living; it's also a means to contribute positively to society and fulfil your potential. The Quran encourages us to strive for excellence in everything we do:

> *"And do good; indeed, Allah loves the doers of good"* - Quran (2:195)

This means setting professional goals that reflect your skills, passions, and the impact you want to have.

Set goals that allow you to grow in your career while also maintaining ethical standards and contributing to the community. For instance, if you're a teacher, your goal might be to develop new teaching methods that help your students excel. If you're in business, you could aim to provide excellent services or products while ensuring fair and honest dealings.

Short-Term and Long-Term Goals

When setting goals, it's helpful to distinguish between short-term and long-term objectives. Short-term goals are the steps you take on a daily, weekly, or monthly basis. Long-term goals are what you aim to achieve over a year or more. Both should be aligned with your personal and professional priorities.

For short-term goals, think about the small actions that lead to bigger changes. This could be daily Quran recitation, regular exercise, or completing a course that enhances your skills.

For long-term goals, consider where you see yourself in the future. Do you want to deepen your knowledge of Islam, advance in your career, or perhaps start a family? These long-term goals give you direction and purpose, helping you stay focused on what truly matters.

Aligning with Islamic Values

Finally, ensure that all your goals are aligned with Islamic values. This means being mindful of your intentions and making sure that your efforts are pleasing to Allah.

Set goals that not only benefit you personally and professionally but also bring you closer to Allah and contribute positively to other

Aligning Goals with Quranic Principles and Life Purpose (Maqasid al-Shariah)

Maqasid al-Shariah refers to the higher objectives or goals of Islamic law. These objectives aim to preserve and protect five essential elements: faith (deen), life (nafs), intellect (aql), progeny (nasl), and wealth (maal). By aligning our goals with these principles, we ensure that our efforts are in harmony with the fundamental tenets of Islam.

Preserving Faith (Deen)

The foremost objective in Islam is to preserve and strengthen our faith. Goals aligned with this principle might include regular prayer, Quranic study, and engaging in community service. The Quran emphasises the importance of worship and remembrance of Allah:

"O you who have believed, remember Allah with much remembrance and exalt Him morning and afternoon." - Quran (33:41-42).

This verse underscores the significance of consistent worship and remembrance of Allah as central to maintaining and strengthening faith.

Setting goals that prioritise your spiritual growth ensures that your faith remains strong and vibrant.

For instance, you might set a goal to attend weekly study circles, memorise specific chapters of the Quran, or volunteer at your local mosque. These activities not only enhance your spiritual life but also foster a sense of community and support.

Protecting Life (Nafs)

Islam places a high value on the sanctity and quality of life. Goals that protect and enhance your physical and mental well-being are crucial. The Quran says:

> *"And do not kill the soul which Allah has forbidden, except by right"* - Quran (17:33)

This principle encourages us to take care of our health and safety.

Your goals might include maintaining a balanced diet, exercising regularly, getting adequate sleep, and managing stress. Additionally, seeking regular medical check-ups and prioritising mental health through mindfulness and stress-relief activities align with this principle.

Cultivating Intellect (Aql)

Islam encourages the pursuit of knowledge and intellectual growth. The Prophet Muhammad (peace be upon him) said:

> *"Whoever takes a path upon which to obtain knowledge, Allah makes the path to Paradise easy for him."* (Sahih Muslim)

Goals that promote learning and intellectual development are highly valued.

Consider setting goals such as reading books on various subjects, attending educational seminars, or pursuing further education. This continuous learning not only enriches your mind but also enhances your ability to contribute positively to society.

Nurturing Progeny (Nasl)

Preserving and nurturing future generations is a key objective in Islam. This includes providing a good upbringing, education, and moral guidance to your children. The Quran highlights the importance of family:

> "O you who have believed protect yourselves and your families from a Fire whose fuel is people and stones" - Quran (66:6)

Goals in this area might include spending quality time with your children, teaching them about Islamic values, and ensuring they receive a good education. Additionally, setting aside time for family activities and creating a supportive home environment are crucial for nurturing future generations.

Safeguarding Wealth (Maal)

The proper management and ethical earning of wealth are essential in Islam. The Quran states:

> "And do not give the weak-minded your property, which Allah has made a means of sustenance for you" - Quran (4:5)

Setting financial goals that include budgeting, saving, and ethical investment ensures that your wealth is managed wisely.

Your goals might involve creating a savings plan, avoiding debt, investing in Halal opportunities, and giving regularly to charity (Zakat and Sadaqah). These practices not only secure your financial future but also fulfil your religious obligations.

Integrating Quranic Principles

Aligning your goals with Quranic principles and Maqasid al-Shariah creates a holistic approach to life. It ensures that your actions are balanced, purposeful, and spiritually enriching. Each goal you set, whether personal or professional, should reflect these divine principles, guiding you towards a life that is pleasing to Allah.

Strategies for Effective Goal Setting

SMART goal-setting approach

Setting goals is one thing, but setting effective goals that you can actually achieve is a whole different ball game. One of the best methods for ensuring your goals are actionable and achievable is the SMART approach. SMART stands for Specific, Measurable, Achievable, Relevant, and Time-bound.

Let's break down how you can use this approach to set goals that align with your Islamic values and lead to meaningful progress, incorporating guidance from the Quran and Hadith.

Specific

The first step in the SMART approach is to make your goals specific. Vague goals are hard to follow and even harder to achieve. A specific goal clearly defines what you want to accomplish. Instead of saying:

"I want to improve my knowledge," be more precise: *"I want to memorise two new Surahs from the Quran within the next three months."*

This specificity gives you a clear target to aim for.

The Quran emphasises clarity and purpose in our actions:

> *"And We have certainly made the Quran easy for remembrance, so is there any who will remember?"* - Quran (54:17)

Being specific helps you focus your efforts and clarifies what you need to do, ensuring your goals are well-defined and purposeful.

Measurable

A goal should be measurable so you can track your progress and know when you've achieved it. This involves defining how you will measure your success. For instance, if your goal is to improve your health, specify how you will measure it: "I want to lose 10 pounds in the next three months by exercising three times a week and following a healthy diet."

Measurable goals allow you to see your progress along the way, providing tangible evidence of your efforts, which can be very motivating.

Achievable

While it's good to aim high, your goals should still be realistic and achievable. Setting goals that are too ambitious can lead to frustration and discouragement. Think about what is feasible given your current situation and resources. If you're new to Quranic studies, it might be more achievable to start with one Surah rather than five.

The Quran advises us to consider our capabilities:

> "Allah does not burden a soul beyond that it can bear" - Quran (2:286)

To determine if your goal is achievable, consider any potential obstacles and plan how you will overcome them. This way, you can set yourself up for success rather than disappointment.

Relevant

Your goals should be relevant to your life and aligned with your values and long-term objectives. In the context of Islamic values, relevant goals should contribute to your personal, spiritual, or professional growth. For example, a relevant goal could be, "I want to volunteer at the local mosque every week to give back to my community and strengthen my faith."

The Quran encourages us to engage in beneficial activities:

"And whatever good you put forward for yourselves - you will find it with Allah. It is better and greater in reward" - *Quran (73:20)*

Relevant goals ensure that you are not wasting your time on activities that do not matter to you, keeping you focused on what truly matters.

Time-bound

Finally, your goals should be time-bound, meaning they should have a deadline. A goal without a time frame can lead to procrastination because there's no sense of urgency. For instance, instead of saying, "I want to read more Islamic books," set a specific time frame: "I want to read three Islamic books over the next six months."

Time-bound goals help you stay on track and ensure that you are making progress, creating a sense of urgency that motivates you to take action now rather than later.

Incorporating Dua (supplication) and reliance on Allah in goal achievement

Dua, or supplication, is a direct line of communication with Allah. It's an opportunity to ask for guidance, support, and blessings in every aspect of our lives. The Prophet Muhammad (peace be upon him) said:

> *"Dua is the essence of worship" (Tirmidhi)*

This underscores the significance of making Dua in our daily lives, especially when setting and striving for goals.

When setting your goals, start with a sincere Dua. Ask Allah to help you set goals that are beneficial for your Dunya (worldly life) and Akhirah (hereafter). For example, you might say: "O Allah, guide me to set goals that are pleasing to You and beneficial to myself and others. Grant me the strength and wisdom to achieve them." This not only sets a positive tone but also aligns your intentions with divine guidance.

Tawakkul: Trusting in Allah

Tawakkul, or reliance on Allah, is a cornerstone of Islamic faith. It's about placing your trust in Allah's plan while making your best effort. The Quran beautifully captures this concept:

> *"And put your trust in Allah, and sufficient is Allah as a disposer of affairs" (Quran 33:3)*

This means that while we plan and work hard, we must also trust that Allah knows what is best for us and will guide us accordingly. Prophet Muhammad (peace be upon him) said:

> *"If you have complete trust in Allah, then He will suffice you as He suffices the birds. They go out in the morning with empty bellies and return in the evening with full bellies"* (Ibn Majah)

This emphasises that Tawakkul doesn't negate taking action, but rather complements it with faith. By trusting in Allah's plan, we can find peace and reduce anxiety, knowing that He will provide for us in unexpected ways.When working towards your goals, maintain a balance between effort and trust. Do your best in planning, executing, and overcoming obstacles, but always remember that success ultimately comes from Allah. This mind-set can reduce anxiety and stress, as you're assured that Allah is in control and has the best plan for you.

Regular Supplication

Make it a habit to regularly include Dua in your daily routine. The Prophet Muhammad (peace be upon him) said:

> *"The best supplication is the supplication on the Day of Arafah, and the best of what I and the prophets before me have said is: 'There is no deity except Allah, alone, without partner'"* (Muwatta Malik)

This shows the importance of regular and consistent supplication.

In your daily prayers, ask Allah for success in your goals. For example, after each Salah, you might say, "O Allah, help me achieve my goals with ease and grant me success that brings me closer to You." Consistent supplication keeps your focus on your goals and reinforces your reliance on Allah's guidance and support.

Gratitude and Reflection

While working towards your goals, take time to reflect on your progress and express gratitude for the milestones you achieve. The Quran emphasises gratitude:

> *"If you are grateful, I will surely increase you [in favour]"* - Quran (14:7)

Thank Allah for the small successes and learn from any setbacks.

Reflecting on your journey helps you stay grounded and mindful of Allah's blessings. It also allows you to reassess your goals and make any necessary adjustments, ensuring that your efforts remain aligned with your intentions and Islamic values.

Integrating Dua and Tawakkul in Goal Achievement

To effectively incorporate Dua and Tawakkul in your goal achievement, follow these steps:

1. **Start with Dua**: Begin your goal-setting process with a sincere supplication for guidance and support.

2. **Plan and Act**: Make detailed plans and take consistent action towards your goals.

3. **Trust in Allah**: While you work hard, maintain trust in Allah's plan and wisdom.

4. **Regular Supplication**: Include specific supplications related to your goals in your daily prayers.

5. **Reflect and Be Grateful**: Regularly reflect on your progress, express gratitude for achievements, and seek forgiveness for any shortcomings.

Chapter Four

Planning and Organisation

Imagine trying to navigate a journey without a map. It's easy to get lost, take wrong turns, or end up miles away from your destination. That's what life can feel like without proper planning and organisation. Planning is a powerful tool that transforms your intentions into actions. It's the bridge between where you are now and where you want to be. Islam places great emphasis on being deliberate and thoughtful about our time and actions. The Prophet Muhammad (peace be upon him) demonstrated this through his meticulous approach to both personal and community affairs. Whether it was preparing for battles, managing resources, or organising community events, his life is filled with examples of strategic planning.

Planning also involves preparing for the unexpected. Life is unpredictable, and even the best-laid plans can go awry. Incorporating flexibility into your schedule allows you to adapt to changes without losing sight of your goals. The Prophet Muhammad (peace be upon him) demonstrated this adaptability, always ready to adjust his plans in response to new challenges and opportunities.

One of the most notable examples of the Prophet's strategic planning was during the Battle of the Trench (Ghazwa al-Khandaq). Faced with a siege by a confederate army, the Prophet (peace be upon him) consulted with his companions and adopted Salman al-Farsi's suggestion to dig a trench around Medina. This proactive planning and preparation were instrumental in defending the city and securing a crucial victory. It shows how foresight and preparation can turn the tide in challenging situations.

Importance of Planning in Islamic Management

Prophetic examples of strategic planning and preparation

The Prophet Muhammad (peace be upon him) was not only a spiritual leader but also an astute planner and strategist. His life is filled with instances where meticulous planning played a crucial role in achieving success and ensuring the well-being of the Muslim community.

The Hijra (Migration to Medina)

One of the most significant examples of strategic planning in the Prophet's life is the Hijra, the migration from Mecca to Medina. Facing increasing persecution in Mecca, the Prophet (peace be upon him) planned the migration meticulously. He selected the right time to leave, took a less-travelled route to avoid detection, and arranged for provisions and guides to ensure a safe journey. This careful planning was instrumental in the successful establishment of the first Islamic state in Medina.

The Quran highlights the importance of preparation and planning:

> *"O you who have believed, take your precaution"* - Quran (4:71)

The Hijra exemplifies this directive, showing how foresight and strategic thinking can lead to significant achievements.

The Battle of the Trench

Another powerful example of the Prophet's strategic planning is the Battle of the Trench (Ghazwa al-Khandaq). When the Quraysh and their allies planned to attack Medina, the Prophet (peace be upon him) consulted his companions and adopted the suggestion of Salman al-Farsi to dig a trench around the city.

This was an unconventional tactic in Arabian warfare but proved highly effective. The trench created a formidable barrier that the enemy forces could not cross, leading to their eventual withdrawal.

This incident demonstrates the Prophet's openness to new ideas and strategic innovation. His willingness to adopt and implement a well-thought-out plan saved Medina from a potentially devastating attack. It underscores the importance of being proactive and thinking ahead to protect and advance the community.

Treaty of Hudaybiyyah

The Treaty of Hudaybiyyah is another example of the Prophet's strategic foresight. Although the terms of the treaty seemed unfavourable to many Muslims, the Prophet (peace be upon him) recognised the long-term benefits.

The treaty established a ten-year peace, allowing Muslims to spread their message without the threat of immediate conflict. This period of peace led to significant growth in the number of Muslims and the eventual conquest of Mecca.

The Quran states:

> *"Indeed, We have given you, [O Muhammad], a clear conquest"* - *Quran (48:1)*

This refers to the eventual victory following the treaty. The Prophet's ability to see the bigger picture and plan for the future highlights the importance of strategic patience and foresight.

Integrating Prophetic Planning into Daily Life

By looking at these examples, we can learn to incorporate strategic planning into our own lives. Whether it's managing daily tasks, setting long-term goals, or preparing for significant life events, planning helps us navigate challenges and make the most of our opportunities. The Prophet Muhammad (peace be upon him) showed that thoughtful preparation and trust in Allah go hand in hand.

His life demonstrates the power of strategic planning and preparation in achieving success and overcoming challenges. By embracing these principles, we can lead more organised, productive, and fulfilling lives, grounded in our faith and trust in Allah's guidance.

Utilising daily, weekly, and monthly planners for effective organisation

Staying organised in today's fast-paced world can be a challenge. That's where planners come in handy. Whether you're managing personal responsibilities, professional tasks, or spiritual commitments, using daily, weekly, and monthly planners can help you stay on track and make the most of your time. In Islam, effective time management is a key principle, and utilising planners aligns perfectly with this ethos.

The Power of Daily Planners

Daily planners are your go-to tool for managing everyday tasks. They help you map out your day in detail, ensuring you don't overlook important duties. Start each day by listing your tasks and appointments. Prioritise them based on their urgency and importance. This practice aligns with the Islamic teaching of prioritising beneficial actions.

The Prophet Muhammad (peace be upon him) said:

> *"The best of deeds are those done regularly, even if they are small" (Sahih Bukhari)*

A daily planner helps you incorporate regular, consistent actions into your routine. Whether it's your daily prayers, work tasks, or time for family, a daily planner ensures you allocate time for each activity.

Structuring Your Week with Weekly Planners

While daily planners help manage your immediate tasks, weekly planners give you a broader view of your commitments. At the start of each week, take some time to outline your main goals and activities. This could include work deadlines, social engagements, and spiritual practices.

Weekly planners are particularly useful for balancing different aspects of life. The Prophet Muhammad (peace be upon him) balanced his time between worship, family, and community affairs. By planning your week, you can ensure you're not neglecting any important areas of your life. It's also a great way to track your progress on longer-term projects.

Monthly Planners for Long-Term Goals

Monthly planners are essential for setting and reviewing long-term goals. At the beginning of each month, identify your key objectives. These could be professional targets, personal development goals, or spiritual aspirations. Break these down into smaller tasks that can be spread out over the weeks.

Using a monthly planner helps you stay focused on your bigger picture. It provides a roadmap for where you want to go and keeps you motivated by showing your progress over time. The Prophet Muhammad (peace be upon him) demonstrated foresight and planning in many aspects of his life, such as the strategic decisions during the migration to Medina and the treaties he established. Similarly, a monthly planner allows you to strategically plan for the future while adapting to any changes that come your way.

Planning for Sacred Months

Incorporating the Islamic sacred months into your planning is crucial. Months like Ramadan and Dhul-Hijjah hold special significance and require additional focus on spiritual activities.

Ramadan: This holy month is a time for fasting, increased prayer, and reflection. The Quran says:

> *"The month of Ramadan [is that] in which was revealed the Quran, a guidance for the people and clear proofs of guidance and criterion"* - Quran (2:185)

Use your daily planner to schedule Suhoor and Iftar times, Taraweeh prayers, and time for Quran recitation. The Prophet Muhammad (peace be upon him) said:

> *"Whoever fasts Ramadan out of faith and in the hope of reward, his previous sins will be forgiven"* (Sahih Bukhari)

Dhul-Hijjah: The first ten days of Dhul-Hijjah are considered the best days of the year for good deeds. The Prophet Muhammad (peace be upon him) said:

> *"There are no days during which righteous deeds are more beloved to Allah than these days" (Sahih Bukhari)*

Plan for increased worship, including fasting on the Day of Arafah. The Quran emphasises the importance of Hajj during this month:

> *"And complete the Hajj and 'umrah for Allah"* - Quran (2:196)

If you're performing Hajj, your monthly planner will be crucial in managing the preparations and rituals.

Integrating Islamic Practices

One of the beautiful aspects of using planners is that you can integrate your spiritual practices seamlessly into your schedule. For instance, you can block out time for your five daily prayers in your daily planner.

In your weekly planner, you might set aside time for attending Jummah prayers or community service. In your monthly planner, you could plan for fasting on the days recommended by the Prophet (peace be upon him) or attending Islamic lectures.

The Quran emphasises the importance of time:

> *"And He it is who made the night and the day in succession for whoever desires to remember or desires gratitude"* - Quran (25:62)

Planners help ensure that your time is used in ways that are pleasing to Allah and beneficial to you.

Reflecting and Adjusting

Another benefit of using planners is the opportunity for reflection. At the end of each day, week, and month, review what you've accomplished and where you might need to adjust. This practice aligns with the Islamic principle of self-accountability. The Prophet Muhammad (peace be upon him) said:

> *"Take account of yourselves before you are taken to account"* (Tirmidhi)

Regular reflection helps you stay on track and make necessary adjustments to your plans. It ensures that you remain focused on your goals and continue to improve your time management skills.

Techniques for Prioritisation and Time Blocking

Eisenhower Matrix for prioritising tasks based on urgency and importance

So how do you decide what needs your immediate attention and what can wait? Enter the Eisenhower Matrix, a simple yet powerful tool for prioritising tasks based on urgency and importance.

This technique can help you manage your time more effectively, ensuring that you focus on what truly matters. Let's dive into how this works and how you can integrate it into your daily routine.

Understanding the Eisenhower Matrix

The Eisenhower Matrix, also known as the Urgent-Important Matrix, helps you categorise tasks into four quadrants:

1. **Urgent and Important**: Tasks that need immediate action. These are your top priorities.

2. **Important but Not Urgent**: Tasks that are important for your long-term goals but don't need immediate attention. Schedule these tasks.

3. **Urgent but Not Important**: Tasks that need to be done quickly but don't contribute significantly to your goals. Delegate these if possible.

4. **Not Urgent and Not Important**: Tasks that are low priority and can be eliminated or postponed.

Applying the Eisenhower Matrix

Quadrant 1: Urgent and Important

These tasks are your top priorities. They often come with deadlines and immediate consequences if not completed. For example, an approaching project deadline at work, an urgent medical appointment, or a critical family matter.

Islam underscores the significance of addressing urgent responsibilities promptly, as expressed in the teachings of the Prophet Muhammad (peace be upon him):

> "The Prophet Muhammad (peace be upon him) said: 'Whoever among you wakes up secure in his property, healthy in his body, and has his food for the day, it is as if he were given the entire world.'" *(Sunan Ibn Majah)*

This hadith highlights the importance of appreciating and making use of your capabilities to fulfil your obligation because you might lose the opportunities presented to you today.

Quadrant 2: Important but Not Urgent

Tasks in this category contribute to your long-term goals and personal growth but don't require immediate action. This could include planning for future projects, investing in self-improvement, or spending quality time with family. Schedule these tasks in your weekly or monthly planner to ensure they get done.

The Quran encourages planning and foresight:

> "And let every soul look to what it has put forth for tomorrow" - Quran (59:18)

By scheduling these important tasks, you ensure that you're continually working towards your goals and not just reacting to immediate demands.

Quadrant 3: Urgent but Not Important

These tasks demand immediate attention but don't significantly impact your long-term objectives. Examples might include attending certain meetings, answering non-critical emails, or handling minor interruptions. If possible, delegate these tasks to others.

The Prophet Muhammad (peace be upon him) was known for delegating tasks to his companions, utilising their strengths to achieve communal goals effectively. This practice not only relieved his burden but also empowered others to contribute.

Quadrant 4: Not Urgent and Not Important

Tasks in this quadrant are often distractions or time-wasters. They don't contribute to your important goals and can often be eliminated. This could include excessive social media use, watching too much TV, or engaging in non-productive activities.

TIME MASTERY

Islam encourages us to be mindful of how we spend our time. The Prophet Muhammad (peace be upon him) said:

"There are two blessings which many people lose: health and free time for doing good" (Sahih Bukhari)

Eliminating or minimising low-priority tasks helps free up time for more meaningful activities.

Integrating Time Blocking

Time blocking is a technique where you allocate specific blocks of time to different tasks or activities. This helps you stay focused and avoid the pitfalls of multitasking. For example, you might block out an hour in the morning for focused work on an important project (Quadrant 2 task) and set aside time in the afternoon for meetings (Quadrant 3 tasks).

The Prophet Muhammad (peace be upon him) demonstrated effective time management in his daily routine, balancing time for worship, family, community, and personal reflection. By following a similar approach, you can ensure that each aspect of your life gets the attention it deserves.

Allocating time blocks for focused work and avoiding multitasking

Multitasking might seem like a good idea to get more done, but it often leads to reduced productivity and increased stress. Allocating specific time blocks for focused work is a powerful technique to enhance productivity and maintain balance in your daily routine. This method aligns well with Islamic principles of intentional and purposeful living.

The Concept of Time Blocking

Time blocking involves dividing your day into distinct blocks of time, each dedicated to a specific task or set of tasks. This approach helps you concentrate on one thing at a time, reducing the inefficiencies of multitasking. By assigning a specific block of time to each task, you can work more efficiently and with greater clarity.

The Pitfalls of Multitasking

Multitasking might seem like an effective way to handle multiple responsibilities, but it often has the opposite effect. Studies have shown that switching between tasks can decrease productivity by up to 40%. It can also lead to increased stress and lower quality of work. In Islam, there is an emphasis on mindfulness and doing things with excellence.

Focusing on one task at a time allows you to put forth your best effort and achieve better results.

How to Allocate Time Blocks

1. **Identify Your Priorities**: Start by listing all the tasks you need to accomplish. Prioritise them based on their importance and urgency. This step aligns with using the Eisenhower Matrix to categorise tasks.

2. **Create a Schedule**: Allocate specific time blocks for each task. For instance, dedicate the first two hours of your day to high-priority tasks that require deep focus. Schedule less demanding tasks for times when your energy levels are lower.

3. **Include Breaks**: Ensure that you schedule short breaks between time blocks. These breaks help you recharge and maintain high levels of productivity throughout the day. The Prophet Muhammad (peace be upon him) encouraged taking breaks, as seen in his practice of dividing the night into por-

tions for prayer, rest, and personal reflection.

4. **Minimise Distractions**: During each time block, minimise distractions by turning off notifications, closing unnecessary tabs on your computer, and setting boundaries with those around you. Informing colleagues or family members of your focus periods can help reduce interruptions.

5. **Review and Adjust**: At the end of each day or week, review your schedule. Reflect on what worked well and what didn't. Adjust your time blocks as needed to better align with your workflow and energy levels.

Integrating Islamic Practices

Integrating time blocking with Islamic practices can further enhance your productivity and spiritual well-being. For example, allocate specific time blocks for your daily prayers (Salat).

These regular breaks for worship not only fulfil religious obligations but also provide moments of reflection and peace, which can enhance your focus and productivity for the rest of the day.

During the month of Ramadan, you might adjust your time blocks to accommodate Suhoor and Iftar, as well as increased time for prayer and Quran recitation. The Quran states:

> *"Indeed, the prayer has been decreed upon the believers a decree of specified times"* - Quran (4:103)

By planning your day around these sacred times, you ensure that your spiritual duties are integrated seamlessly into your schedule.

Benefits of Time Blocking

1. **Enhanced Focus**: By dedicating specific time blocks to single tasks, you can work more efficiently and with greater concentration.

2. **Reduced Stress**: Knowing that you have allocated time for each task helps reduce anxiety about not having enough time.

3. **Better Work Quality**: Focusing on one task at a time allows you to put forth your best effort, resulting in higher quality work.

4. **Increased Productivity**: Structured time blocks help you make the most of your day, leading to greater overall productivity.

Chapter Five

Time Management Tools and Resources

Balancing our time between different roles and responsibilities can be challenging. However, both the Quran and the Hadith provide valuable insights into achieving this balance.

The Prophet Muhammad (peace be upon him) was known for his meticulous planning and ability to manage various aspects of life effectively. By drawing inspiration from his practices, we can learn to allocate our time in ways that fulfil our duties and enrich our lives.

In today's digital age, technology offers numerous tools to assist us in managing our time more efficiently. From apps that organise tasks to digital calendars that remind us of prayer times, integrating these tools into our daily routine can help us stay organised and focused on our goals.

Utilising technology in a way that supports our spiritual and practical needs can significantly enhance our productivity and spiritual well-being.

Reflection and Self-Assessment

Quranic verses for self-reflection and improvement

Self-reflection is about taking a step back and looking at our lives objectively. It involves analysing our actions, understanding our motivations, and assessing whether we are living in accordance with our values and beliefs. The Quran emphasises the significance of this introspective practice:

> *"And the soul and He who proportioned it. And inspired it with discernment of its wickedness and its righteousness. He has succeeded who purifies it, and he has failed who instills it [with corruption]." - Quran (91:7-10)*

This verse reminds us to regularly examine our deeds and their implications for our future. By doing so, we can ensure that our actions contribute positively to our spiritual journey and prepare us for the Hereafter.

Quranic Verses for Self-Reflection and Improvement

Several verses in the Quran specifically encourage self-reflection and provide guidance on how to improve ourselves. Here are a few key verses:

Accountability and Personal Responsibility

> *"And every soul will be fully compensated [for] what it did; and He is most knowing of what they do." - Quran (39:70)*

This verse highlights the importance of personal accountability. Reflecting on our actions helps us understand that we are responsible for our deeds and their consequences. By acknowledging our shortcomings, we can take proactive steps to improve and seek Allah's forgiveness.

Contemplating Life and Death

> *"Every soul will taste death. And you will only be given your [full] compensation on the Day of Resurrection. So he who is drawn away from the Fire and admitted to Paradise has attained [his desire]. And what is the life of this world except the enjoyment of delusion." - Quran (3:185)*

Reflecting on the transient nature of life and the certainty of death can motivate us to focus on what truly matters. This contemplation encourages us to prioritise our spiritual well-being and strive for actions that bring us closer to Allah.

Seeking Forgiveness and Repentance

> *"And those who, when they commit an immorality or wrong themselves [by transgression], remember Allah and seek forgiveness for their sins – and who can forgive sins except Allah? – and [who] do not persist in what they have done while they know." - Quran (3:135)*

Self-reflection allows us to recognise our mistakes and seek forgiveness. The process of repentance and seeking Allah's mercy is a crucial aspect of self-improvement. It helps us cleanse our hearts and renew our commitment to living righteously.

The Reminder of Self-Reproach

> *"Nay, man will be a witness against himself, even if he presents his excuses." - Quran (75:14-15)*

This verse from Surah Al-Qiyamah emphasises the role of self-awareness and self-accountability. It reminds us that we are our own best witnesses to our actions and intentions. Even if we try to justify our shortcomings, deep down, we know where we stand. This awareness is the first step towards genuine self-improvement.

Practical Steps for Self-Reflection

1. **Daily Reflection**: Set aside a few minutes each day to reflect on your actions. Consider what you did well and where you could improve. This practice helps you stay mindful of your behaviour and its alignment with Islamic values.

2. **Journaling**: Writing down your thoughts and reflections can provide clarity and insight. Use a journal to record your daily reflections, goals, and progress. This habit allows you to track your growth over time and make necessary adjustments.

3. **Prayer and Meditation**: Engage in regular prayer and meditation to connect with Allah and seek guidance. Use these moments of spiritual reflection to ask for strength and wisdom in overcoming your shortcomings.

4. **Accountability Partner**: Consider finding a trusted friend or mentor with whom you can share your reflections and seek advice. An accountability partner can provide support, encouragement, and constructive feedback.

Evaluating time usage based on Quranic teachings

Islam places a strong emphasis on tadabbur (deep reflection) and fikr (contemplation). The Quran frequently reminds us of the significance of time and the need to use it wisely. One of the most poignant reminders is found in Surah Al-Asr:

> *"O you who have believed, let not your wealth and your children divert you from remembrance of Allah. And whoever does that - then those are the losers. And spend [in the way of Allah] from what We have provided you before death approaches one of you and he says, 'My Lord, if only You would delay me for a brief term so I would give charity and be among the righteous.'"* - Quran (63:9-10)

This verse highlights that every moment we have is an opportunity to engage in meaningful and righteous activities. To avoid being among those who are "in loss," we must continuously assess how we are utilising our moments through deep reflection and contemplation

Self-assessment as a means of personal growth is crucial in Islam. The Quran states:

> *"And those who, when they commit an immorality or wrong themselves [by transgression], remember Allah and seek forgiveness for their sins—and who can forgive sins except Allah?—and [who] do not persist in what they have done while they know."* - Quran (3:135)

Assessing our daily routines and how they align with our spiritual and personal aspirations involves regularly questioning whether our actions are bringing us closer to Allah and fulfilling our duties. Islam guides us to find harmony between our worldly responsibilities and spiritual commitments. The Quran teaches:

> *"Indeed, the hereafter is better for you than the first [life]."* - Quran (93:4)

This verse reminds us to keep our ultimate focus on the Hereafter while engaging in worldly activities. By thoughtfully distributing our time among work, family, self-improvement, and worship, we can lead a balanced and rewarding life.

At the end of each day, set aside a few minutes for tadabbur and fikr, reflecting on how you spent your time. Identify activities that were productive and aligned with your goals, and recognise areas for improvement. Keeping a journal to track your daily activities and reflections can provide insights into patterns and help you make informed adjustments to your schedule. Use tools like the Eisenhower Matrix to prioritise tasks based on their urgency and importance, ensuring that your moments are spent on meaningful activities.

Time Allocation Strategies

The Quran and Hadith provide us with timeless wisdom on how to allocate our time effectively, ensuring that we fulfil our responsibilities in a balanced and meaningful way. By following these teachings, we can manage our time in a manner that enhances both our worldly and spiritual lives.

Quranic Examples of Balanced Time Allocation

The Quran provides clear guidance on balancing our time between worship, work, and personal responsibilities. One of the fundamental verses on time management is:

> *"But seek, through that which Allah has given you, the home of the Hereafter; and [yet], do not forget your share of the world. And do good as Allah has done good to you. And desire not corruption in the land. Indeed, Allah does not like corrupters."* - Quran (28:77)

This verse emphasises the need to balance our pursuit of the Hereafter with our responsibilities in this world. It highlights that while our ultimate goal should be the Hereafter, we must not neglect our worldly duties. This balanced approach ensures that we are contributing positively to society while also focusing on our spiritual growth.

The story of Prophet Ibrahim (Abraham) is another excellent example of balanced time allocation. He was deeply devoted to Allah, yet he also fulfilled his duties as a family man and a leader. His life teaches us the importance of dedicating time to worship, family, and community, demonstrating that one can successfully manage multiple roles without neglecting any.

Prophetic Guidance on Managing Various Life Roles Effectively

The Prophet Muhammad (peace be upon him) was a perfect example of balanced time management. He fulfilled his roles as a prophet, leader, husband, father, and friend, demonstrating how to manage various responsibilities effectively. His daily routine was a testament to his ability to balance different aspects of life.

Balancing Worship and Daily Responsibilities

The Prophet Muhammad (peace be upon him) was meticulous in his prayer times, ensuring that he never missed his obligatory prayers. He emphasised the importance of prayer as a means of connecting with Allah and recharging spiritually. However, he also understood the importance of fulfilling worldly duties. He said:

> *"The strong believer is better and more beloved to Allah than the weak believer, while there is good in both" (Sahih Muslim)*

This hadith underscores the importance of being strong and capable in both spiritual and worldly matters.

Time for Family and Social Responsibilities

The Prophet (peace be upon him) was known for his compassion and dedication to his family. He spent quality time with his wives, played with his children, and cared for his relatives. His relationship with his family members was characterised by love, respect, and understanding.

This highlights the importance of allocating time for family, ensuring that they receive the care and attention they deserve.

Community Engagement

The Prophet (peace be upon him) also dedicated significant time to his community. He was actively involved in social issues, provided guidance, and resolved disputes. His leadership style was inclusive and compassionate, showing that effective time management includes contributing to the well-being of the community. He advised:

> *"Whoever relieves a Muslim of some distress in this world, Allah will relieve him of some distress on the Day of Resurrection" (Sahih Muslim)*

This underscores the importance of community service and social responsibility.

Practical Steps for Balanced Time Allocation

1. **Set Clear Priorities**: Identify your key responsibilities and prioritise them. Ensure that your spiritual duties, family obligations, and work commitments are all accounted for in your daily schedule.

2. **Create a Schedule**: Develop a daily and weekly schedule that includes time for prayer, work, family, and personal activities. Stick to this schedule as closely as possible to maintain balance.

3. **Integrate Worship**: Incorporate your prayer times into your daily routine. Use these moments to pause, reflect, and reconnect with Allah, ensuring that your spiritual duties are not neglected.

4. **Quality Family Time**: Allocate specific times for family activities. Engage in meaningful conversations, play with your children, and ensure that your family feels valued and loved.

5. **Community Involvement**: Dedicate time each week to participate in community activities. Volunteer, attend community events, and contribute to social welfare projects.

6. **Regular Reflection**: At the end of each day, reflect on how you spent your time. Assess whether you managed to balance your responsibilities effectively and identify areas for improvement.

Utilising Technology for Time Management

From organising tasks and schedules to incorporating reminders for prayer times, there are numerous apps and digital tools that can help us stay on track. For Muslims, these tools not only assist in maintaining productivity but also ensure that spiritual duties are integrated seamlessly into daily routines.

Let's explore some recommended apps and digital tools for effective time management and how to incorporate Islamic reminders into our digital calendars.

Recommended Apps and Digital Tools for Organising Tasks and Schedules

Todoist

Todoist is a versatile task management app that allows you to create and organise tasks with ease. You can set deadlines, prioritise tasks, and even collaborate with others. Its intuitive interface makes it easy to track your progress and stay focused on your goals.

Google Calendar

Google Calendar is a widely-used scheduling tool that integrates well with other Google services. It allows you to schedule events, set reminders, and share your calendar with others. You can create multiple calendars for different aspects of your life, such as work, personal, and spiritual activities.

Trello

Trello is a visual project management tool that uses boards, lists, and cards to help you organise tasks. It's particularly useful for managing complex projects and collaborating with teams. You can create boards for different projects and use lists to track tasks from start to finish.

Microsoft Outlook

Microsoft Outlook combines email and calendar functions, making it a comprehensive tool for managing your schedule. It offers features such as event scheduling, task management, and email integration, all in one place. This can be especially useful for professionals who need to juggle multiple responsibilities.

Notion

Notion is an all-in-one workspace that combines note-taking, task management, and project planning. It allows you to create customised templates and databases to organise your tasks and projects. Its flexibility makes it suitable for both personal and professional use.

Incorporating Islamic Reminders and Prayer Times into Digital Calendars

Muslim Pro

Muslim Pro is a comprehensive Islamic app that offers prayer times, Quran recitations, and other religious resources. It provides accurate prayer times based on your location and sends notifications for each prayer. You can integrate Muslim Pro with your digital calendar to ensure you never miss a prayer.

Athan

Athan is another popular Islamic app that provides prayer times, Quran verses, and Islamic content. It offers customisable prayer time notifications and can be synced with your calendar. This ensures that you are reminded of your prayer obligations throughout the day.

Google Calendar Integration

To incorporate prayer times into Google Calendar, you can manually add the prayer times as recurring events. Alternatively, you can use third-party services that automatically sync prayer times with your Google Calendar. This integration allows you to have a holistic view of your daily schedule, including both your professional and spiritual commitments.

Iqama

Iqama is a simple app designed to help Muslims keep track of their prayer times. It sends notifications for each prayer and allows you to customise the reminder settings. By syncing Iqama with your digital calendar, you can ensure that your daily prayers are integrated into your overall schedule.

Dua & Azkar

Dua & Azkar is an app that provides daily supplications and reminders for important Islamic practices. It offers a variety of duas for different occasions and sends notifications to remind you to recite them. Integrating these reminders into your digital calendar can help you stay spiritually connected throughout the day.

Practical Tips for Effective Use of Technology in Time Management

1. Customise Your Tools

Choose the apps and tools that best fit your needs and customise them to suit your preferences. Set up notifications and reminders that help you stay on track without overwhelming you.

2. Integrate and Sync

Ensure that all your digital tools are integrated and synced. This allows you to have a unified view of your tasks and schedules, making it easier to manage your time effectively.

3. Set Boundaries

While technology can be a great aid, it's important to set boundaries to avoid digital overload. Allocate specific times for checking emails and social media, and stick to these times to maintain a healthy balance.

4. Regularly Review and Adjust

Periodically review your digital setup to ensure it's still meeting your needs. Adjust your notifications, reminders, and schedules as necessary to keep everything running smoothly.

5. Stay Mindful

Use your digital tools to support your goals and values. Incorporate reminders for spiritual practices, such as prayer and reflection, to ensure that your use of technology enhances your overall well-being.

Benefits of Time Tracking and Analysis

Monitoring Productivity and Identifying Time-Wasting Activities

Time tracking involves recording how each minute of your day is spent. Tools and apps like Toggl, Clockify, or even simple spreadsheets can be used for this purpose. The aim is to gain a clear understanding of where your time goes, which is the first step towards making meaningful changes.

When you start tracking your time, you might be surprised at how much is spent on non-essential activities. This could include excessive social media use, prolonged email checking, or unproductive meetings. Identifying these time-wasting activities is crucial for self-improvement. Regular self-assessment helps us stay aligned with our goals and responsibilities.

Improvements Based on Data-Driven Insights

Once you have data on how your time is spent, analyse it to identify areas for improvement. Data-driven insights can help you make informed decisions about optimising your schedule and increasing productivity.

For example, if you notice that too much time is spent on low-priority tasks, you can adjust your schedule to focus more on high-priority activities. Techniques like the Eisenhower Matrix can help prioritise tasks based on urgency and importance. Time blocking can ensure uninterrupted periods for important work.

Time tracking also helps identify patterns in productivity. You may find that you are most productive at certain times of the day. Scheduling your most important tasks during these peak periods ensures that you are using your energy and focus efficiently.

Additionally, time tracking supports a balanced life, which is a key Islamic principle. By observing how much time you dedicate to work, family, personal growth, and spiritual practices, you can make necessary adjustments. The Quran advises:

> *"And do not make your hand [as] chained to your neck or extend it completely and [thereby] become blamed and insolvent." - Quran (17:29)*

This verse emphasises the importance of moderation and balance in all aspects of life, encouraging us to wisely manage our resources and time.

Chapter Six

Dealing with Time Wasters

We live in an age where distractions are abundant. From endless social media scrolling to binge-watching TV shows, these activities can easily consume large chunks of our time without us even realising it. The Quran and Hadith offer profound guidance on avoiding such frivolous pursuits and emphasise the importance of utilising our time wisely. Understanding and acknowledging these time-wasting habits is the first step toward reclaiming our time and redirecting it towards more beneficial activities.

The Quran often reminds us of the transient nature of this world and the importance of preparing for the Hereafter. Surah Al-Asr, for instance, succinctly captures this essence:

> *"Until, when death comes to one of them, he says, 'My Lord, send me back that I might do righteousness in that which I left behind.' No! It is only a word he is saying; and behind them is a barrier until the Day they are resurrected." - Quran (23:99-100)*

This verse serves as a powerful reminder that every moment counts and should be used to engage in activities that bring us closer to Allah and benefit others.

The Prophet Muhammad (peace be upon him) was a paragon of time management. His life exemplified how to balance various responsibilities while ensuring that time was utilised efficiently.

Practical tips such as setting clear goals, prioritising tasks, and creating structured routines can significantly reduce the time spent on non-essential activities. Additionally, adopting a mindful approach to time management—where we are fully aware of how each moment is spent—aligns our actions with our values and long-term objectives.

Identifying Common Time-Wasting Habits

In our modern world, distractions are abundant. Common time-wasting habits include excessive social media use, mindless internet browsing, binge-watching TV shows, and engaging in idle gossip. These activities can consume large portions of our day, leaving us with little time for meaningful and productive tasks. The first step towards reclaiming our time is to recognise and acknowledge these habits.

Quranic Teachings on Avoiding Frivolous Activities

The Quran provides clear guidance on the importance of using time wisely and avoiding frivolous activities. In Surah Al-Asr, Allah swears by time to emphasise its significance:

> *"Know that the life of this world is but amusement and diversion and adornment and boasting to one another and competition in increase of wealth and children - like the example of a rain whose [resulting] plant growth pleases the tillers; then it dries and you see it turned*

> *yellow; then it becomes [scattered] debris. And in the Hereafter is severe punishment and forgiveness from Allah and approval. And what is the worldly life except the enjoyment of delusion."* - Quran (57:20)

This powerful verse highlights that many aspects of worldly life are distractions and emphasises the importance of focusing on actions that bring us closer to Allah and benefit others. This calls for a mindful approach to how we spend our time, avoiding frivolous pursuits.

The Quran also cautions against idle talk and frivolous activities. In Surah Al-Mu'minun, successful believers are described as those:

> *"Who are humble in their prayers; and who turn away from ill speech."* - Quran (23:2-3)

Avoiding "laghw" (vain talk) is essential for a believer. This includes not just idle gossip but any activity that distracts us from our primary purpose of worship and fulfilling our responsibilities.

In contrast, those who are distracted and waste their time are often described in the Quran with warnings and admonitions. For instance, in Surah Al-Kahf, Allah speaks about those whose efforts are wasted in this worldly life:

> *"Say, 'Shall We inform you of the greatest losers in their deeds? [They are] those whose effort is lost in worldly life, while they think that they are doing well in work.'"* - Quran (18:103-104)

This verse serves as a stern reminder that engaging excessively in worldly pursuits without purpose can lead to a great loss, even if one believes they are doing well.

Prophetic Guidance on Utilising Time Wisely

The Prophet Muhammad (peace be upon him) is the epitome of efficient time management. His life offers a blueprint for how to balance various roles and responsibilities while making the most of every moment. He consistently emphasised the importance of using time wisely.

The Prophet Muhammad (peace be upon him) said:

> *"An hour in the morning or evening spent in the path of Allah is better than the world and whatever is in it."*
> *(Sahih Muslim)*

This hadith highlights the immense value of dedicating time to acts of worship and righteous deeds. It encourages believers to prioritise their actions and invest their time in activities that bring them closer to Allah and benefit others. By seizing opportunities to perform good deeds, individuals can accumulate spiritual rewards that surpass worldly possessions and achievements. This aligns with the Islamic principle of utilising time wisely and focusing on actions that have lasting significance in both this life and the Hereafter.

The Prophet Muhammad (peace be upon him) also advised against idle activities and encouraged productive use of time. He said:

> *"The feet of the son of Adam will not move from near his Lord on the Day of Judgment until he is asked about five things: about his life – how he spent it; his youth – how he took care of it; his wealth – how he earned it; how he spent it; and what he did with his knowledge."*
> *(Tirmidhi)*

TIME MASTERY

This hadith reminds us that we will be held accountable for how we spend our time. It emphasises the need to be mindful and intentional about our activities.

The Essence of a Mindful Believer

A mindful believer is characterised by intentionality and purpose in their actions. They are conscious of the transient nature of life and strive to use their time in ways that are pleasing to Allah and beneficial to themselves and others. The Quran and Hadith repeatedly highlight the qualities of such believers.

In Surah Al-Mu'minoon, Allah says:

> "And those who carefully maintain their prayer: They will be in gardens, honored." - Quran (23:9-11)

This verse underscores that those who make a conscious effort to use their time for the sake of Allah will be guided and supported by Him. This divine support is a powerful motivator for believers to avoid time-wasting activities and focus on righteous deeds.

Practical Steps to Avoid Time-Wasting Habits

1. **Set Clear Goals**: Define what you want to achieve in your personal, professional, and spiritual life. Clear goals help you stay focused and avoid distractions.

2. **Prioritise Tasks**: Use tools like the Eisenhower Matrix to prioritise tasks based on their importance and urgency. This ensures that you are working on what truly matters.

3. **Schedule Regular Reflection**: Set aside time each day or week to reflect on how you are using your time. Assess whether your activities are aligned with your goals and values.

4. **Engage in Beneficial Activities**: Focus on activities that contribute to your growth and well-being, such as learning, volunteering, and spending time with family.

5. **Limit Distractions**: Identify your main sources of distraction and take steps to minimise them. This might involve setting limits on social media use, creating a dedicated workspace, or establishing specific times for checking emails.

Strategies to Eliminate Time-Wasters

Practical Tips for Minimising Distractions and Time-Consuming Habits

Identify Your Time Wasters

The first step in eliminating time wasters is to identify them. Reflect on your daily activities and pinpoint those that consume time without adding value to your life. Common time wasters include excessive use of social media, watching TV, browsing the internet aimlessly, and engaging in idle gossip. The Quran warns against frivolous activities:

> *"Successful indeed are the believers. Those who humble themselves in their prayers; who avoid vain talk"* - Quran (23:1-3)

Set Clear Goals and Priorities

Having clear goals and priorities is crucial for staying focused and avoiding distractions. Write down both short-term and long-term goals, then break them into manageable tasks. Prioritise these tasks using tools like the Eisenhower Matrix, which categorises them into urgent and important, important but not urgent, urgent but not important, and neither urgent nor important.

This structured approach helps you make the most of your time, aligning with the Quranic wisdom that emphasises mindfulness and purpose in all actions.

Create a Structured Schedule

Develop a daily and weekly schedule that includes time for work, family, personal growth, and spiritual practices. Allocate specific time blocks for each activity, and stick to your schedule as closely as possible.

This structured approach helps ensure that all important aspects of your life receive adequate attention. Regularly scheduled breaks for prayer (Salah) can serve as natural pauses in your day, allowing you to reflect and refocus.

Use Technology Wisely

While technology can be a significant source of distraction, it can also be a powerful tool for time management if used wisely. Utilise apps and digital tools that help you organise tasks and schedules.

For instance, Todoist and Trello can help you manage your to-do lists and projects, while Google Calendar can keep your schedule organised. Additionally, apps like Muslim Pro and Athan can provide reminders for prayer times, ensuring that your spiritual duties are integrated into your daily routine.

Limit Social Media and Internet Use

Set specific times for checking social media and browsing the internet, and stick to these limits. Consider using website blockers or apps that restrict access to distracting websites during work hours. The Quran advises moderation in all aspects of life:

> *"And those who, when they spend, are neither extravagant nor miserly, but hold a medium (way) between those (extremes)"* - Quran (25:67)

Applying this principle to your internet use can help you avoid wasting time.

Create a Distraction-Free Workspace

Designate a specific area in your home or office for focused work. Ensure that this space is free from distractions, such as noise and clutter. Inform family members or colleagues of your working hours to minimise interruptions.

The Prophet Muhammad (peace be upon him) emphasised the importance of creating an environment conducive to productivity:

> *"Allah loves that whenever any of you does something, he does it perfectly"* (Al-Bayhaqi)

Practice Mindful Task Management

Focus on one task at a time, and give it your full attention. Multitasking can lead to reduced productivity and increased stress. By concentrating on a single task, you can complete it more efficiently and with higher quality.

The Quran encourages mindfulness and intentionality in our actions:

> *"And whatever you do of good – indeed, Allah is Knowing of it"* - Quran (2:197)

Regularly Review and Reflect

Set aside time at the end of each day or week to review your activities and reflect on how you spent your time. Identify areas where you can improve and make necessary adjustments to your schedule. The Quran emphasises the importance of self-assessment:

> *"O you who have believed, fear Allah as He should be feared and do not die except as Muslims [in submission to Him]. And hold firmly to the rope of Allah all together and do not become divided."* - Quran (3:102-103)

Developing a Mindful Approach to Time Management

Cultivate Self-Awareness

Mindful time management begins with self-awareness. Be conscious of how you spend your time and the impact of your activities on your overall well-being. Self-awareness allows you to make intentional choices about how to allocate your time. The Quran advises believers to reflect and be mindful:

> *"Indeed, in the creation of the heavens and the earth and the alternation of the night and the day are signs for those of understanding. Who remember Allah while standing or sitting or [lying] on their sides and give thought to the creation of the heavens and the earth, [saying], 'Our Lord, You did not create this aimlessly;*

exalted are You [above such a thing]; then protect us from the punishment of the Fire'" - *Quran (3:190-191)*

Integrate Spiritual Practices

Incorporate regular spiritual practices into your daily routine. Prayer (Salah), Quran recitation, and Dhikr (remembrance of Allah) provide moments of reflection and connection with Allah. These practices not only fulfil religious obligations but also serve as breaks that rejuvenate and refocus your mind.

> *"Whoever performs ablution like this ablution of mine and then offers two Rak'ahs (units of prayer) without allowing his thoughts to be distracted, all his previous sins will be forgiven." (Sahih Bukhari)*

By incorporating these spiritual practices into your daily routine, you ensure that your faith remains a central part of your life, providing spiritual nourishment and balance.

Practice Gratitude

Gratitude is a powerful tool for mindful living. Regularly expressing gratitude for the time and opportunities you have can help you appreciate each moment and use it wisely. The Quran encourages gratitude:

> *"And [remember] when your Lord proclaimed: 'If you are grateful, I will surely increase you [in favor]; but if you deny, indeed, My punishment is severe'"* - *Quran (14:7)*

Set Intentions

Begin each day with a clear intention of what you aim to achieve. Setting intentions helps you stay focused and aligned with your goals. The Prophet Muhammad (peace be upon him) said,

> "Verily, Allah does not look at your forms or wealth, but rather He looks at your hearts and actions." (Sahih Muslim)

This hadith highlights that Allah judges us based on our intentions and actions rather than outward appearances or material possessions. It encourages believers to ensure their intentions are sincere and their actions are aligned with the teachings of Islam.

By setting intentions, you can ensure that your actions are purposeful and meaningful.

Embrace Simplicity

Simplify your life by focusing on what truly matters. Eliminate unnecessary tasks and commitments that do not contribute to your goals or well-being. The Quran advises:

> *"And do not obey one whose heart We have made heedless of Our remembrance and who follows his desire and whose affair is ever [in] neglect."* - Quran (18:28)

Embracing simplicity allows you to allocate your time more effectively and reduce stress.

Mindful Transitions

Be mindful of transitions between tasks. Take a moment to pause and reset your mind before moving on to the next activity. This practice helps maintain focus and prevents the accumulation of mental fatigue. The Prophet Muhammad (peace be upon him) demonstrated mindfulness in his actions, always being present and intentional in his interactions and activities.

Seek Continuous Improvement

Strive for continuous improvement in how you manage your time. Regularly seek feedback, learn from your experiences, and make adjustments to your approach. The Quran emphasises the value of learning and growth:

> *"And say, 'My Lord, increase me in knowledge'"* - *Quran (20:114)*

Embracing a mind-set of continuous improvement helps you refine your time management skills and achieve greater productivity.

Chapter Seven

Balancing Work, Worship, and Rest

Islam calls for excellence (Ihsan) in every aspect of life, whether in worship or work. Performing acts of worship with sincerity and striving for excellence in our professional duties can transform our daily grind into acts of devotion. This chapter explores how to achieve a balance between our worldly responsibilities and spiritual commitments, highlighting the profound sense of fulfilment that comes from consistent worship and mindful living.

Balancing work, worship, and rest is about more than just managing time; it's about aligning our actions with our values and priorities. Islam teaches us that success in this world and the Hereafter are not mutually exclusive but rather intertwined goals. By embracing the concept of Ihsan and integrating spiritual practices into our daily routines, we can achieve a harmonious and fulfilling life.

Work-Life Balance in Islam

Islam places a significant emphasis on maintaining a balance between our worldly duties and spiritual responsibilities. The Quran provides clear guidance on how to achieve this balance, encouraging believers to seek the Hereafter while not neglecting their share of this world.

Quranic References on Balancing Worldly Pursuits with Spiritual Obligations

One of the most profound verses on this subject is:

> *"And when the prayer has been concluded, disperse within the land and seek from the bounty of Allah, and remember Allah often that you may succeed."* - Quran (62:10)

This verse beautifully encapsulates the essence of work-life balance in Islam. It reminds us that while we should strive for success in the Hereafter, we must also take care of our responsibilities in this world. The key is to strike a balance where neither aspect is neglected.

Another verse that emphasises the importance of balancing our worldly and spiritual lives is:

> *"O you who have believed, let not your wealth and your children divert you from remembrance of Allah. And whoever does that - then those are the losers."* - Quran (63:9)

This verse serves as a warning against allowing our worldly pursuits, such as earning wealth and raising families, to distract us from our primary obligation of remembering and worshiping Allah. It highlights the need for mindful living, where we ensure that our spiritual obligations remain a priority.

Fostering a Holistic Approach to Time Management

To achieve a balance between work and worship, it is crucial to adopt a holistic approach to time management. This involves integrating our spiritual practices into our daily routines, setting clear priorities, and being mindful of how we spend our time.

Setting Clear Priorities

Start by setting clear priorities that align with your values and long-term goals. Make a list of your responsibilities and categorise them into spiritual, personal, and professional domains. This helps in understanding where your time and energy need to be focused.

For instance, your spiritual priorities might include daily prayers (Salah), Quran recitation, and engaging in Dhikr (remembrance of Allah). Personal priorities could involve spending quality time with family, taking care of your health, and pursuing hobbies. Professional priorities would cover work-related tasks and career development.

Once you have a clear understanding of your priorities, it becomes easier to allocate time and energy accordingly. This ensures that no single aspect of your life overshadows the others, helping you maintain a balanced and fulfilling lifestyle.

Integrating Spiritual Practices

Integrating spiritual practices into your daily routine is essential for maintaining a strong connection with Allah and ensuring that your faith remains central to your life. Here are some practical ways to achieve this:

1. **Daily Prayers (Salah)**: Schedule your daily prayers around your work and personal activities. Use prayer times as breaks to pause, reflect, and reconnect with Allah. This not only fulfils your spiritual obligations but also provides mental and emo-

tional rejuvenation.

2. **Quran Recitation**: Dedicate specific times each day for reading and reflecting on the Quran. This could be in the morning before starting your day or in the evening before bed. Consistent Quran recitation helps you stay connected to the divine message and provides guidance in your daily life.

3. **Dhikr (Remembrance of Allah)**: Incorporate moments of Dhikr throughout your day. Whether you are commuting, taking a walk, or doing household chores, silently remembering Allah keeps you spiritually grounded and mindful.

Time Management Techniques

Adopting effective time management techniques can help you balance your work and spiritual obligations more efficiently. Here are some strategies to consider:

1. **Time Blocking**: Allocate specific blocks of time for different activities. For example, set aside time in the morning for personal development and spiritual practices, dedicate the middle of the day to professional tasks, and reserve the evening for family and relaxation.

2. **Pomodoro Technique**: This technique involves working in focused intervals (usually 25 minutes) followed by short breaks. Use these breaks for quick prayers or moments of Dhikr, ensuring that your spiritual practices are woven into your workday.

3. **Eisenhower Matrix**: Prioritise tasks based on their urgency and importance. This helps you focus on what truly matters and avoid getting bogged down by less significant activities. Ensure that your spiritual obligations are categorised as high-priority tasks.

Maintaining Work-Life Boundaries

Maintaining clear boundaries between work and personal life is crucial for achieving balance. Here are some tips to help you maintain these boundaries:

1. **Set Specific Work Hours**: Define your work hours and stick to them. Avoid letting work spill over into your personal time. This helps you ensure that you have dedicated time for family, relaxation, and spiritual practices.

2. **Create a Dedicated Workspace**: If possible, create a dedicated workspace that is separate from your living areas. This physical separation helps reinforce the boundary between work and personal life.

3. **Unplug After Work**: Make a conscious effort to unplug from work-related activities after your designated work hours. Avoid checking work emails or taking work calls during your personal time.

The Role of Rest

Rest and relaxation are essential components of a balanced life. Islam recognises the importance of rest and encourages believers to take care of their bodies and minds. The Prophet Muhammad (peace be upon him) emphasised the importance of balance and rest, stating:

> *"Your body has a right over you, your eyes have a right over you, and your wife has a right over you." (Sahih Bukhari)*

Ensuring that you get adequate rest and relaxation helps you recharge and maintain your overall well-being. This, in turn, enables you to fulfil your spiritual and professional responsibilities more effectively.

Integrating Salah (Prayer) into Daily Routine

Importance of Observing Salah at Prescribed Times

Salah is one of the Five Pillars of Islam and serves as a direct link between the believer and Allah. The Quran repeatedly emphasises the significance of observing prayers at their appointed times:

> *"Indeed, prayer has been decreed upon the believers a decree of specified times."* - Quran (4:103)

Observing Salah at its prescribed times ensures that the spiritual benefits of prayer are fully realised. These benefits include:

Spiritual Rejuvenation

Salah provides regular intervals throughout the day to reconnect with Allah, offering moments of peace and reflection. This spiritual rejuvenation strengthens faith and reinforces the believer's commitment to Islamic principles.

Mental Clarity and Focus

Prayer helps clear the mind of distractions and stresses, allowing for improved concentration and mental clarity. This mental reset can enhance productivity and decision-making.

Discipline and Time Management

Adhering to the specific times for Salah instils discipline and encourages effective time management. It ensures that no matter how busy life gets, moments are dedicated to spiritual reflection and worship.

Strategies for Maintaining Focus and Productivity Around Prayer Times

Balancing work, personal responsibilities, and Salah requires thoughtful planning and discipline. Here are some strategies to help maintain focus and productivity while ensuring that prayer times are observed:

Plan Your Day Around Salah

Schedule your daily activities around the five prayer times. By prioritising Salah and making it the anchor points of your day, you can create a rhythm that balances work and worship. For example, plan work sessions between Fajr and Dhuhr, and use the time after Dhuhr for meetings or tasks that require more energy.

Use Prayer Times as Breaks

Treat Salah times as natural breaks during your day. These breaks not only fulfil your religious obligations but also provide opportunities to rest and recharge. Studies show that taking regular breaks can improve productivity and mental well-being.

Set Reminders

Use alarms or app notifications to remind you of upcoming prayer times. Apps like Muslim Pro and Athan offer customisable prayer time alerts, ensuring you never miss a Salah. These reminders help you pause your activities and prepare for prayer.

Create a Conducive Environment

Establish a quiet and clean space for prayer, free from distractions. This dedicated space can enhance the quality of your Salah and help you maintain focus during prayer. If you're at work, find a suitable place where you can pray without interruptions.

Mindful Transitioning

Prepare for Salah by gradually transitioning from your current activity. Spend a few moments clearing your mind and making the intention (niyyah) for prayer. This mindful approach helps you enter a state of calmness and devotion.

Integrating Salah and Dhikr into Daily Schedules

Incorporating Salah and Dhikr into your daily routine goes beyond merely performing the obligatory prayers. It involves embedding these spiritual practices into the fabric of your everyday life, ensuring continuous connection with Allah.

Morning Routine with Fajr and Dhikr

Start your day with Fajr prayer, followed by a few minutes of Dhikr or Quran recitation. This sets a positive tone for the day, filling it with spiritual energy and purpose. The Prophet Muhammad (peace be upon him) said:

> *"The two Rak'ahs before the dawn (Fajr) prayer are better than this world and all it contains" (Sahih Muslim)*

Midday Recharge with Dhuhr and Dhikr

Use the time after Dhuhr prayer for a brief period of Dhikr or Quran study. This midday spiritual boost can enhance your focus and productivity for the rest of the day. Incorporating short moments of reflection and gratitude during this time can also be beneficial.

Afternoon Focus with Asr

Asr prayer serves as a perfect transition from the busy part of the day to the evening. It's a time to pause, reflect on the day's progress, and refocus your intentions. This break can help you approach the latter part of the day with renewed energy and clarity.

Evening Reflection with Maghrib and Dhikr

After Maghrib prayer, take a moment to reflect on the day's accomplishments and seek forgiveness for any shortcomings. Engaging in Dhikr during this time helps you wind down and prepares your mind for a peaceful evening.

Night-time Peace with Isha and Dhikr

End your day with Isha prayer, followed by a few minutes of Dhikr or Quran recitation. This night-time routine ensures that you close your day on a spiritual note, seeking Allah's protection and guidance for the night and the day to come.

Integrate Dhikr Throughout the Day

Beyond the structured prayer times, incorporate moments of Dhikr into your daily activities. Whether you are commuting, taking a walk, or doing household chores, silently remembering Allah keeps you spiritually grounded and mindful.

Embracing the Concept of Ihsan (Excellence) in Work and Worship

Performing Acts of Worship with Sincerity and Excellence (Ihsan)

The essence of Ihsan in worship is to perform every act with a deep sense of sincerity and excellence. The Prophet Muhammad (peace be upon him) described Ihsan as:

> *"To worship Allah as if you see Him, and if you do not see Him, He surely sees you" (Sahih Muslim)*

This profound understanding transforms every act of worship into an intimate and purposeful experience.

Sincerity in Worship

Sincerity (Ikhlas) is fundamental to Ihsan. When performing acts of worship, it is crucial to do so purely for the sake of Allah, without seeking recognition or reward from others. The Quran emphasises the importance of sincerity:

> *"And they were not commanded except to worship Allah, [being] sincere to Him in religion, inclining to truth, and to establish prayer and to give zakah. And that is the correct religion." - Quran (98:5)*

This verse reminds us that the foundation of our faith is sincere worship. Whether it's praying, fasting, giving charity, or any other act of devotion, it should be done with the sole intention of pleasing Allah.

Excellence in Worship

Excellence in worship means striving to perform our religious duties with the utmost care and precision. This includes understanding the proper way to perform prayers, reciting the Quran with Tajweed (correct pronunciation), and maintaining cleanliness and humility. The Prophet Muhammad (peace be upon him) said:

> *"Allah loves that when any one of you does a job, he does it perfectly."* (Al-Bayhaqi)

Applying this principle to our acts of worship means continuously seeking to improve and perfect our religious practices. This dedication not only enhances the quality of our worship but also deepens our connection with Allah.

Achieving Balance Between Worldly Responsibilities and Spiritual Commitments

Balancing worldly responsibilities with spiritual commitments is a challenge that many Muslims face. However, the concept of Ihsan provides a framework to manage both effectively, ensuring that neither is neglected.

Prioritising Responsibilities

To achieve this balance, it is essential to prioritise responsibilities. Start by identifying your primary obligations in both realms. For instance, fulfilling the five daily prayers and other religious duties should be non-negotiable aspects of your schedule. At the same time, meeting work deadlines and family commitments are crucial for maintaining a balanced life.

By integrating both aspects into our daily lives, we can achieve a holistic balance.

Time Management and Planning

Effective time management is key to balancing work and worship. Develop a daily schedule that allocates specific times for work, family, personal development, and spiritual practices. Tools such as planners, calendars, and time-blocking techniques can help ensure that all important areas of life receive adequate attention.

Set aside time for Salah, Quran recitation, and Dhikr within your daily routine. These moments of spiritual connection can serve as breaks that rejuvenate and refocus your mind, enhancing overall productivity.

Finding Spiritual Fulfilment Through Consistent Worship

Consistent worship is not only a duty but also a source of immense spiritual fulfilment. By maintaining regularity in our acts of worship and striving for Ihsan, we can experience profound spiritual growth and satisfaction.

Regularity and Consistency

The Prophet Muhammad (peace be upon him) emphasised the importance of consistency in worship:

> *"The most beloved deeds to Allah are those that are done regularly, even if they are small." (Sahih Bukhari)*

Consistency in worship fosters a strong and enduring connection with Allah. It helps build discipline and ensures that spiritual practices become an integral part of our daily lives.

Deepening Spiritual Connection

Regular and sincere worship deepens our spiritual connection with Allah. It allows us to experience His presence in our lives, providing comfort, guidance, and strength. The Quran encourages believers to remember Allah frequently:

> "O you who have believed, remember Allah with much remembrance and exalt Him morning and afternoon." - Quran (33:41-42)

Engaging in regular Dhikr and Quran recitation, along with Salah, enhances our awareness of Allah and brings tranquillity to our hearts.

Spiritual Reflection and Growth

Consistent worship also provides opportunities for spiritual reflection and growth. By regularly assessing our intentions and actions, we can identify areas for improvement and seek Allah's guidance in becoming better Muslims. The process of self-reflection and repentance is integral to spiritual development:

> "O you who have believed, fear Allah. And let every soul look to what it has put forth for tomorrow – and fear Allah. Indeed, Allah is Acquainted with what you do." - Quran (59:18)

This verse emphasises the importance of self-assessment and accountability, encouraging believers to continuously strive for excellence in their faith.

Practical Tips for Embracing Ihsan in Daily Life

1. **Set Clear Intentions**: Before performing any act of worship or daily task, set a clear intention (niyyah) to do it for the sake of Allah. This aligns your actions with your spiritual goals and enhances their significance.

2. **Seek Knowledge**: Continuously seek knowledge about your faith and how to perform acts of worship correctly. Attend religious classes, read Islamic literature, and seek guidance from knowledgeable individuals.

3. **Create a Conducive Environment**: Establish a peaceful and clean environment for worship. This can help you focus and perform your religious duties with greater concentration and sincerity.

4. **Incorporate Dhikr into Daily Activities**: Make Dhikr a part of your daily routine by remembering Allah during mundane tasks such as commuting, cooking, or exercising. This practice keeps you spiritually grounded throughout the day.

5. **Reflect and Repent**: Regularly reflect on your actions and seek Allah's forgiveness for any shortcomings. This process of reflection and repentance helps you stay mindful of your spiritual journey and motivates continuous improvement.

Chapter Eight

Overcoming Procrastination and Laziness

The Quran and Hadith provide valuable insights into why we procrastinate and how we can combat this tendency. By recognising the psychological barriers and spiritual aspects of procrastination, we can develop a comprehensive approach to overcoming it.

The Quran addresses the human tendency to delay important tasks, emphasising the importance of taking timely action. For instance, Allah says:

> *"And hasten to forgiveness from your Lord and a garden as wide as the heavens and earth, prepared for the righteous"* - Quran (3:133)

This verse encourages believers to act promptly in seeking forgiveness and striving for righteousness, highlighting the urgency of good deeds.

Moreover, the Prophet Muhammad (peace be upon him) frequently sought refuge in Allah from laziness and procrastination. He used to recite a specific dua:

> *"O Allah, I seek refuge in You from anxiety and sorrow, weakness and laziness, miserliness and cowardice, the burden of debts and from being overpowered by men (other people)" (Sahih Bukhari)*

This supplication reflects the importance of seeking divine help in overcoming these negative traits.

Addressing procrastination involves tackling both psychological and spiritual barriers. Psychological factors such as fear of failure, lack of motivation, and poor time management can contribute to procrastination. Spiritually, procrastination can stem from a weak connection with Allah and a lack of mindfulness about the transient nature of life.

Understanding the Causes of Procrastination in Islamic Context

Understanding the Causes of Procrastination in Islamic Context

Understanding the causes of procrastination from an Islamic perspective involves examining Quranic teachings, addressing psychological barriers and spiritual aspects, and seeking refuge in Allah through specific duas. This comprehensive approach can help individuals overcome procrastination and lead more productive and spiritually fulfilling lives.

Quranic Perspectives on Procrastination

The Quran provides numerous insights into the importance of time and the dangers of wasting it. Procrastination, which involves delaying tasks and decisions, is implicitly warned against in several verses. The

Quran emphasises the value of immediate action, particularly in the context of good deeds and seeking forgiveness.

One of the most poignant verses regarding the urgency of righteous actions is found in Surah Adh-Dhariyat:

> *"So flee to Allah. Indeed, I am to you from Him a clear warner."* - Quran (51:50)

This verse highlights the fleeting nature of time and the inevitable loss faced by those who do not use it wisely. It underscores the importance of belief, righteous deeds, truth, and patience—all of which require timely action.

Another verse that emphasises the need for immediate action is:

> *"And hasten to forgiveness from your Lord and a garden as wide as the heavens and earth, prepared for the righteous."* - Quran (3:133)

This verse encourages believers to seek Allah's forgiveness and strive for Paradise without delay. The use of the word "hasten" signifies the urgency and importance of acting promptly in spiritual matters.

The Quran also warns against being distracted by worldly pursuits, which can lead to procrastination in fulfilling spiritual obligations:

> *"O you who have believed, let not your wealth and your children divert you from remembrance of Allah. And whoever does that - then those are the losers."* - Quran (63:9)

This verse highlights how distractions, such as wealth and family, can lead to neglecting the remembrance of Allah. It serves as a reminder to prioritise spiritual duties over worldly distractions.

Addressing Psychological Barriers and Spiritual Aspects of Procrastination

Procrastination can stem from various psychological barriers and spiritual deficiencies. Understanding these underlying causes is essential for addressing and overcoming procrastination effectively.

Psychological Barriers

1. **Fear of Failure**: Many people procrastinate because they fear failing at the tasks they need to complete. This fear can paralyse them, leading to avoidance behaviours. Islam teaches that reliance on Allah (Tawakkul) and trusting in His wisdom can help overcome this fear.

2. **Lack of Motivation**: A lack of intrinsic motivation can lead to procrastination. Setting clear, achievable goals and understanding the spiritual significance of tasks can boost motivation. The Prophet Muhammad (peace be upon him) emphasised the importance of intention (niyyah) in all actions, which can help align one's motivations with Islamic values.

3. **Perfectionism**: The desire to perform tasks perfectly can lead to procrastination, as individuals may delay starting a task due to fear that it will not meet their high standards. Islam encourages striving for excellence (Ihsan) but also recognises human limitations, teaching that Allah values sincere efforts.

4. **Poor Time Management**: Ineffective time management can lead to procrastination. The Quran and Hadith provide guidance on the wise use of time, such as the importance of structuring one's day around the five daily prayers (Salah), which

can serve as a natural framework for time management.

Spiritual Aspects

1. **Weak Connection with Allah**: A weak spiritual connection can lead to procrastination in religious duties. Strengthening one's relationship with Allah through regular prayer, Quran recitation, and Dhikr (remembrance of Allah) can foster a sense of urgency and purpose.

2. **Neglecting the Reality of Death and Hereafter**: Procrastination can result from ignoring the transient nature of life and the certainty of death. The Quran frequently reminds believers of the Hereafter and the need to prepare for it. Reflecting on these realities can motivate prompt action.

3. **Lack of Spiritual Discipline**: Spiritual discipline involves regular, consistent worship and adherence to Islamic principles. Developing this discipline can combat laziness and procrastination. It encourages believers to set regular times for prayer, Quran recitation, and other acts of worship. By doing so, we create a routine that keeps us focused and spiritually aligned. Regular worship and reflection help reinforce this discipline, making it easier to stay committed to our spiritual and worldly responsibilities.

Seeking Refuge in Allah from Procrastination (Dua for Overcoming Laziness)

In addition to understanding the causes of procrastination and addressing them, seeking refuge in Allah through specific supplications (duas) is a powerful tool for overcoming laziness. The Prophet Muhammad (peace be upon him) regularly sought Allah's help in overcoming negative traits, including laziness.

One of the most well-known duas for seeking refuge from laziness is:

"O Allah, I seek refuge in You from anxiety and sorrow, weakness and laziness, miserliness and cowardice, the burden of debts and from being overpowered by men (other people)." (Sahih Bukhari)

This dua encompasses various negative traits that can hinder productivity and spiritual growth. By regularly reciting this supplication, believers acknowledge their dependence on Allah and seek His assistance in overcoming these obstacles.

Another relevant dua is:

"O Allah, help me to remember You, to thank You, and to worship You in the best manner." (Sunan Abi Dawood)

This supplication seeks Allah's aid in maintaining mindfulness, gratitude, and excellence in worship—all of which are essential for combating procrastination.

Practical Steps to Overcome Procrastination

Combining spiritual guidance with practical strategies can effectively combat procrastination. Here are some steps to help integrate these insights into daily life:

1. **Set Clear Intentions (Niyyah)**: Begin each task with a clear intention to please Allah. This aligns your actions with your spiritual goals and provides intrinsic motivation.

2. **Break Tasks into Smaller Steps**: Large tasks can be overwhelming, leading to procrastination. Break them into smaller, manageable steps and tackle each step individually. Celebrate small successes to maintain motivation.

3. **Use Time Management Tools**: Utilise tools such as planners, calendars, and to-do lists to organise your tasks and manage your time effectively. Schedule your day around the five daily prayers to ensure a balanced and structured routine.

4. **Practice Mindfulness (Muraqaba)**: Regularly practice mindfulness to stay present and focused. This can involve short sessions of Dhikr or reflective prayer, helping you remain connected to your spiritual goals.

5. **Seek Accountability**: Share your goals and progress with a trusted friend or mentor who can provide encouragement and hold you accountable. The Prophet Muhammad (peace be upon him) encouraged believers to support one another in righteous deeds.

6. **Reflect on the Hereafter**: Regularly remind yourself of the transient nature of life and the importance of preparing for the Hereafter. Reflecting on death and the Day of Judgment can instil a sense of urgency and purpose.

7. **Recite Relevant Duas**: Incorporate the supplications mentioned earlier into your daily routine. Regularly seeking Allah's help in overcoming laziness and procrastination reinforces your reliance on Him.

Techniques for Overcoming Procrastination

Implementing the 5-Second Rule and Other Motivational Strategies

The 5-second rule, popularised by Mel Robbins, is a simple yet powerful technique to combat procrastination. It involves counting down from five and then immediately taking action on the task at hand. This method helps to interrupt patterns of hesitation and push oneself into action before the brain can create excuses to delay. In the context of Islamic teachings, you can combine this with Dhikr (remembrance of Allah) to ensure that your actions are spiritually grounded. For example, before starting a task, say "Bismillah" (In the name of Allah) and then count down "5-4-3-2-1" and begin.

In addition to the 5-second rule, other motivational strategies can be highly effective:

Visualise Success

Imagine the positive outcomes of completing the task. Visualising success can create a mental image of achievement and motivate you to act. The Prophet Muhammad (peace be upon him) said:

> *"Guard over that which benefits you, seek Allah's help, and do not lose heart.." (Sahih Muslim)*

This hadith encourages believers to be proactive, seek Allah's help, and maintain a positive mindset even in challenging situations. It indirectly highlights the importance of visualising success by focusing on productive actions and trusting in Allah's decree.

Align your visualisations with your spiritual intentions.

Set Small Goals

Break larger tasks into smaller, manageable goals. Achieving these smaller milestones provides a sense of accomplishment and keeps you motivated. The Prophet (peace be upon him) emphasised the importance of taking consistent, small steps towards larger goals:

> *"The deeds most loved by Allah are those done regularly, even if they are small." (Sahih Muslim)*

Reward Yourself

Establish a reward system for completing tasks. Small rewards can provide extra motivation and make the process more enjoyable. Rewards should be wholesome and permissible (Halal) to ensure they align with Islamic principles.

Seeking Accountability Through Support Networks and Partnerships

Accountability is a powerful tool in overcoming procrastination. The concept of mutual support and community is deeply rooted in Islam. The Prophet Muhammad (peace be upon him) said:

> *"Help your brother, whether he is an oppressor or he is oppressed." When asked, "It is right to help him if he is oppressed, but how should we help him if he is an oppressor?" He replied, "By preventing him from oppressing others." (Sahih Bukhari)*

This hadith highlights the importance of supporting and being supported by others, encouraging us to seek and provide accountability in our actions.

Accountability Partners

Find a trusted friend, family member, or colleague who can serve as your accountability partner. Share your goals and progress with them regularly. They can provide encouragement, offer constructive feedback, and help you stay on track.

Support Groups:

Join or form a support group with individuals who share similar goals. Regular meetings or check-ins can create a supportive environment where members motivate each other to stay productive.

Public Commitments

Make your goals known publicly, whether through social media or within your community. Public commitments increase the pressure to follow through and reduce the likelihood of procrastination.

Islamic teachings emphasise the importance of community and mutual support. By involving others in your goals and progress, you create a sense of responsibility and external motivation.

Practical Tips Derived from the Sunnah for Overcoming Procrastination

The Sunnah of the Prophet Muhammad (peace be upon him) offers numerous practical tips for overcoming procrastination. His life exemplified discipline, productivity, and a strong sense of purpose. Here are some actionable tips derived from his practices:

Start the Day Early

The Prophet (peace be upon him) encouraged beginning the day early. He said:

> *"O Allah, bless my nation in their early mornings (i.e., what they do early in the morning)" (Sunan Ibn Majah)*

Starting the day early allows for more productive hours and helps avoid the rush and stress that can lead to procrastination.

Maintain a Structured Routine

Having a regular routine can enhance productivity and reduce procrastination. The Prophet (peace be upon him) maintained a structured daily schedule that balanced worship, work, and personal activities. Implementing a similar routine can provide clarity and purpose for each part of the day.

Prioritise Tasks

The Prophet (peace be upon him) taught the importance of prioritising tasks. He would often complete the most important duties first, ensuring that critical responsibilities were addressed promptly. Identify and prioritise your tasks based on their significance and urgency.

Seek Refuge from Laziness

Regularly recite the dua for seeking refuge from laziness:

> *"O Allah, I seek refuge in You from laziness, miserliness and cowardice, the burden of debts, and from being overpowered by men (other people)" (Sahih Bukhari)*

This supplication can help you stay mindful of the need to remain active and engaged.

Practice Consistency

The Quran emphasises the value of consistent actions, stating:

> *"So remain on a right course as you have been commanded, [you] and those who have turned back with you [to Allah], and do not transgress. Indeed, He is Seeing of what you do." (Quran 11:112)*

This verse emphasises the importance of maintaining a consistent and righteous path as commanded by Allah.

Consistency builds habits and reduces the likelihood of procrastination.

Cultivating a Proactive Mind-set in Accordance with Islamic Teachings

A proactive mind-set involves taking initiative, being forward-thinking, and acting with a sense of purpose. Islamic teachings provide a strong foundation for cultivating such a mind-set, emphasising the importance of action, diligence, and reliance on Allah.

Embrace Tawakkul (Reliance on Allah)

Tawakkul means placing complete trust in Allah while also taking necessary actions. It combines proactive effort with faith in Allah's plan. The Quran states:

> "And whoever relies upon Allah – then He is sufficient for him" (Quran 65:3)

This balance encourages believers to act decisively while trusting in Allah's wisdom.

Reflect on the Temporary Nature of Life

Regularly contemplate the transient nature of this world and the inevitability of the Hereafter. The Quran reminds us,

> "What is the life of this world but amusement and play? But verily the Home in the Hereafter—that is life indeed, if they only knew" (Quran 29:64)

TIME MASTERY

Reflecting on this reality can instil a sense of urgency and motivate proactive behaviour.

Set Intentions (Niyyah) for Actions

Begin each task with a clear intention to please Allah. This aligns your efforts with spiritual goals and imbues your actions with purpose.

Setting sincere intentions can transform mundane tasks into acts of worship.

Regular Self-Assessment (Muraqabah)

Practice regular self-assessment to evaluate your actions and progress. Reflect on your achievements, identify areas for improvement, and set new goals. The Quran advises:

> *"O you who have believed, fear Allah and seek the means [of nearness] to Him and strive in His cause that you may succeed." (Quran 5:35)*

This practice helps maintain accountability and fosters continuous improvement..

Incorporate Dhikr (Remembrance of Allah)

Make Dhikr a regular part of your daily routine. Engaging in the remembrance of Allah helps maintain spiritual awareness and keeps you focused on your goals. The Quran encourages frequent Dhikr:

> *"O you who have believed, remember Allah with much remembrance" (Quran 33:41)*

Engage in Continuous Learning

Strive for continuous personal and spiritual growth. Seek knowledge, attend classes, and read Islamic literature to enhance your understanding and skills. The Prophet (peace be upon him) said:

> *"Seeking knowledge is an obligation upon every Muslim" (Sunan Ibn Majah)*

Chapter Nine

Delegation and Collaboration

Delegation, or Wakalah, is the process of entrusting responsibilities to others. In Islam, this practice is essential for fostering leadership, empowering individuals, and ensuring that tasks are completed efficiently.

The Quran and Hadith provide numerous examples of delegation, where leaders entrusted capable individuals with significant responsibilities, thereby promoting a culture of trust and accountability. By examining these examples, we can learn how to delegate effectively, balancing trust (Amanah) with accountability to achieve optimal results.

Collaboration, on the other hand, involves working together towards common goals. Islam places great emphasis on unity, cooperation, and mutual support. The concept of Shura (consultation) encourages collective decision-making, recognising the value of diverse perspectives and talents.

Effective collaboration harnesses the collective strengths of team members, leading to innovative solutions and a cohesive, productive environment. By fostering a culture of teamwork, we can ensure that everyone feels valued and motivated to contribute their best efforts.

The Prophet Muhammad (peace be upon him) demonstrated the power of delegation and collaboration through his leadership. He appointed governors, military leaders, and administrators, empowering them to manage their respective domains while providing guidance and support.

This strategic delegation not only ensured the smooth functioning of the Muslim community but also developed the leadership skills of his companions. Similarly, the Prophet (peace be upon him) emphasised the importance of working together, likening the believers to a single body, where the well-being of each part affects the whole.

Importance of Delegating Responsibilities in Islam

Prophetic Examples of Delegation and Empowerment (Wakalah)

The Prophet Muhammad (peace be upon him) demonstrated exemplary leadership by delegating responsibilities to his companions, thereby empowering them and ensuring the efficient functioning of the Muslim community.

His approach to delegation was not only practical but also strategic, aimed at developing the skills and capabilities of those around him.

Delegation in Governance and Administration

One of the most notable examples of delegation by the Prophet (peace be upon him) is his appointment of governors and administrators to manage different regions. For instance, he appointed Mu'adh ibn Jabal as the governor of Yemen, entrusting him with both administrative and judicial responsibilities. Before Mu'adh departed, the Prophet (peace be upon him) gave him guidance on how to govern, emphasising justice and adherence to Islamic principles.

This delegation allowed the Prophet (peace be upon him) to ensure that the community's needs were met while also fostering leadership skills in his companions.

Delegation in Military Affairs

The Prophet (peace be upon him) also delegated military leadership to capable individuals. During the Battle of Mu'tah, he appointed Zaid ibn Harithah as the commander of the Muslim army. If Zaid were to fall, he appointed Ja'far ibn Abi Talib, and if Ja'far were to fall, Abdullah ibn Rawahah was to take over.

This clear chain of command ensured that the army remained organised and focused, even in the face of adversity. This delegation of military responsibilities highlights the Prophet's foresight and his ability to empower others to lead.

Delegation in Community and Social Services

In the daily affairs of the community, the Prophet (peace be upon him) delegated tasks to various companions, each according to their strengths and capabilities. For example, he appointed Bilal ibn Rabah as the Mu'adhdhin (the caller to prayer), recognising his melodious voice and strong faith.

This delegation not only ensured that the call to prayer was performed beautifully but also honoured Bilal's unique talent.

Empowerment Through Delegation

Delegation in Islam is not merely about distributing tasks; it is about empowering individuals and recognising their potential. The Prophet (peace be upon him) delegated responsibilities in a manner that developed leadership qualities and a sense of accountability among his companions.

This empowerment is evident in how the Prophet (peace be upon him) treated his companions with respect and trust, often seeking their advice and involving them in decision-making processes.

The Quran supports the concept of consultation and shared responsibility:

> *"And those who have responded to their lord and established prayer and whose affair is [determined by] consultation among themselves, and from what We have provided them, they spend."* - Quran (42:38)

This verse highlights the importance of collective decision-making and the distribution of responsibilities, fostering a collaborative and empowered community.

Balancing Trust (Amanah) and Accountability in Delegation

Delegation is a vital aspect of effective leadership and management, deeply rooted in Islamic principles. The practice of delegating responsibilities, or Wakalah, involves not only assigning tasks but also balancing trust (Amanah) and accountability. In Islam, trust is a profound concept that encompasses responsibility, honesty, and ethical conduct. Balancing this trust with accountability ensures that delegated tasks are performed with integrity and efficiency, aligning with Islamic values.

The Concept of Amanah (Trust)

Amanah, or trust, is a core principle in Islam, representing a divine responsibility bestowed upon individuals. It signifies the trust that Allah places in humans to act justly and responsibly in all aspects of life. The Quran emphasises the importance of fulfilling this trust:

> *"Indeed, Allah commands you to render trusts to whom they are due and when you judge between people to judge with justice. Excellent is that which Allah instructs you. Indeed, Allah is ever Hearing and Seeing."* - Quran (4:58)

This verse underscores the significance of fulfilling responsibilities with fairness and integrity. When delegating tasks, it is crucial to ensure that the individuals entrusted with these responsibilities are capable and trustworthy.

Prophetic Guidance on Balancing Trust and Accountability

The Prophet Muhammad (peace be upon him) exemplified the balance between trust and accountability in his leadership. He delegated tasks to his companions, trusting them to perform their duties with diligence and integrity. However, he also established systems of accountability to ensure that these tasks were carried out effectively.

Trust in Delegation

The Prophet (peace be upon him) demonstrated immense trust in his companions by assigning them significant responsibilities. For example, he appointed Abu Bakr as the leader of prayers in his absence, showing confidence in his spiritual and leadership abilities. This act of trust not only empowered Abu Bakr but also reinforced the importance of Amanah in leadership.

Accountability in Delegation

While trust is essential, it must be balanced with accountability to ensure that tasks are performed correctly and efficiently. The Prophet (peace be upon him) held his companions accountable for their actions and provided guidance when necessary. For instance, he would seek reports from appointed leaders and governors to ensure that their actions aligned with Islamic principles and community needs.

An example of this balance is seen in the appointment of Mu'adh ibn Jabal as the governor of Yemen. Before Mu'adh departed, the Prophet (peace be upon him) advised him on how to govern justly and asked him about his approach to decision-making.

This interaction demonstrated trust in Mu'adh's abilities while also establishing a framework for accountability.

Practical Steps for Balancing Trust and Accountability

1. **Select the Right Individuals**: When delegating tasks, choose individuals who are trustworthy, capable, and aligned with Islamic values. Assess their skills and integrity to ensure they can handle the responsibilities entrusted to them.

2. **Provide Clear Guidance**: Clearly communicate the expectations, goals, and standards for the delegated tasks. Providing guidance ensures that the individual understands their responsibilities and the importance of fulfilling them with excellence.

3. **Establish Accountability Mechanisms**: Implement systems for monitoring progress and providing feedback. Regular check-ins, progress reports, and constructive feedback help maintain accountability and support the individual in performing their duties effectively.

4. **Encourage Transparency and Honesty**: Foster an environment where individuals feel comfortable sharing challenges and seeking assistance. Transparency and honesty are crucial for maintaining trust and ensuring that tasks are completed with integrity.

5. **Acknowledge and Reward Efforts**: Recognise and reward the efforts and achievements of those to whom responsibilities have been delegated. Acknowledgment reinforces the value of their contributions and motivates them to continue performing their duties diligently.

The Prophet Muhammad (peace be upon him) exemplified this balance through his leadership, demonstrating that trust and accountability are not mutually exclusive but rather complementary. Embrace these principles in your leadership and management practices, ensuring that your actions reflect the values of trust and accountability, and contribute to a harmonious and productive environment.

Building Effective Teams and Collaborative Partnerships

Leveraging collective strengths and talents for shared goals

One of the key aspects of building effective teams is recognising and utilising the diverse strengths and talents of each member. In Islam, the concept of Shura (consultation) encourages collective decision-making and collaboration. The Quran highlights the importance of consultation and teamwork:

> *"And those who have responded to their lord and established prayer and whose affair is [determined by] consultation among themselves, and from what We have provided them, they spend."* - Quran (42:38)

This verse underscores the significance of involving team members in decision-making processes and leveraging their unique skills and perspectives for the benefit of the collective.

Identifying and Utilising Strengths

Effective team building starts with identifying the strengths and talents of each member. This can be done through regular assessments, feedback sessions, and open communication. By understanding the unique abilities and expertise of each individual, leaders can assign roles and responsibilities that align with their strengths, ensuring that tasks are performed efficiently and effectively.

For instance, in a community project, someone with strong organisational skills can be tasked with planning and coordination, while a person with excellent communication skills can handle outreach and public relations. By aligning tasks with individual strengths, teams can achieve higher levels of productivity and satisfaction.

Encouraging Collaboration and Cooperation

Islamic teachings emphasise the importance of working together and supporting one another. The Prophet Muhammad (peace be upon him) said:

> *"A believer to another believer is like a building whose different parts enforce each other." The Prophet then clasped his hands with the fingers interlaced (while saying that). (Sahih Bukhari)*

This hadith highlights the interconnectedness of the Muslim community and the importance of mutual support and cooperation. In a team setting, fostering a culture of collaboration involves:

1. **Open Communication**: Encourage open and honest communication among team members. Create an environment where everyone feels comfortable sharing their ideas, concerns, and feedback.

2. **Shared Vision and Goals**: Clearly define the team's vision and goals, ensuring that all members understand and are committed to achieving them. This shared purpose helps unite the team and directs their efforts towards common objectives.

3. **Trust and Respect**: Build trust and respect among team members by promoting ethical behaviour, transparency, and mutual respect. Trust is the foundation of effective teamwork and collaboration.

4. **Conflict Resolution**: Establish mechanisms for resolving conflicts constructively. Encourage members to address issues promptly and seek solutions that are fair and beneficial for all.

5. **Recognition and Appreciation**: Recognise and appreciate the contributions of each team member. Celebrate successes and milestones, and provide constructive feedback to help members grow and improve.

Leveraging Diversity

Diversity is a strength that can enhance team performance and innovation. Islam encourages embracing diversity and learning from one another. The Quran states:

> *"O mankind, indeed We have created you from male and female and made you peoples and tribes that you may know one another. Indeed, the most noble of you in the sight of Allah is the most righteous of you. Indeed, Allah is Knowing and Acquainted." - Quran (49:13)*

By leveraging diverse backgrounds, experiences, and perspectives, teams can develop more creative solutions and make better-informed decisions. Embracing diversity also fosters inclusivity and unity, which are core Islamic values.

Communicating expectations clearly and fostering a culture of teamwork

Clear communication is foundational for any successful team. In an Islamic context, the importance of clarity in communication is highlighted in various teachings and practices. The Quran emphasises the value of clear and straightforward speech:

> *"O you who have believed, fear Allah and speak words of appropriate justice."* - Quran (33:70)

This verse underscores the importance of speaking clearly and justly, which can be applied to setting and communicating expectations within a team.

Practical Steps for Clear Communication

1. **Define Roles and Responsibilities**: Clearly outline the roles and responsibilities of each team member. This helps avoid confusion and ensures that everyone knows what is expected of them. Detailed job descriptions and regular updates on individual tasks can enhance understanding.

2. **Set Specific Goals and Objectives**: Establish clear, measurable goals for the team. Specific objectives provide a roadmap for what needs to be achieved and help keep everyone aligned and focused. Use tools like SMART goals (Specific, Measurable, Achievable, Relevant, Time-bound) to ensure clarity.

3. **Regular Meetings and Check-ins**: Hold regular team meetings to discuss progress, address any issues, and provide updates. These check-ins allow for open communication and help keep everyone on the same page.

4. **Written Communication**: Follow up verbal communication with written summaries. This can include meeting minutes, emails, or shared documents that outline decisions and action items. Written records ensure that everyone has a clear reference point.

5. **Feedback Mechanisms**: Implement systems for giving and receiving feedback. Constructive feedback helps team members understand how they are performing and where they can improve. Encourage a two-way feedback process to promote openness and growth.

Fostering a Culture of Teamwork

A culture of teamwork is characterised by collaboration, trust, and mutual respect. Islam emphasises the importance of working together and supporting one another, as reflected in the teachings of the Prophet Muhammad (peace be upon him).

Practical Steps to Foster Teamwork

1. **Promote Mutual Respect**: Encourage team members to respect each other's opinions, strengths, and contributions. A culture of respect fosters a positive and inclusive environment where everyone feels valued.

2. **Encourage Collaboration**: Create opportunities for team members to work together on projects and tasks. Collaborative efforts can lead to innovative solutions and a stronger sense of unity. Use team-building activities to strengthen bonds.

3. **Recognise and Celebrate Successes**: Acknowledge individual and team achievements. Celebrating successes boosts morale and reinforces the value of teamwork. Public recognition and rewards can motivate team members to continue

working collaboratively.

4. **Provide Support and Resources**: Ensure that team members have the necessary resources and support to perform their tasks effectively. This includes training, tools, and access to information. Providing support demonstrates a commitment to the team's success.

5. **Lead by Example**: Leaders play a crucial role in fostering a culture of teamwork. By demonstrating collaborative behaviour, open communication, and mutual respect, leaders set the tone for the rest of the team.

Chapter Ten

Stress Management and Resilience

In today's high-paced world, stress and adversity seem to be constant companions. Whether it's work pressures, personal challenges, or global uncertainties, managing stress effectively and building resilience are more important than ever. Islam, with its profound spiritual teachings and practical guidance, offers a comprehensive approach to dealing with stress and fostering resilience.

Drawing from the wisdom of the Quran and the practices of the Prophet Muhammad (peace be upon him), this chapter explores how we can find peace and strength amidst life's trials.

From seeking refuge in patience and prayer to incorporating mindfulness and physical activities into our routines, Islamic teachings provide a rich tapestry of methods for stress management.

The Prophet Muhammad (peace be upon him), who faced immense challenges throughout his life, serves as an exemplary model of resilience. His methods of coping with stress—rooted in deep faith, steadfastness, and practical action—offer timeless lessons for modern-day struggles.

Prophetic Methods of Coping with Stress and Adversity

Seeking refuge in patience (Sabr) and prayer during times of stress

The Prophet Muhammad (peace be upon him) faced numerous trials and tribulations throughout his life, yet he consistently demonstrated remarkable resilience and unwavering faith. His approach to coping with stress and adversity serves as a timeless guide for Muslims seeking to navigate life's challenges with grace and strength. Two key strategies that the Prophet (peace be upon him) employed were seeking refuge in patience (Sabr) and prayer (Salah).

Patience (Sabr) as a Shield Against Stress

Patience, or Sabr, is a central concept in Islam that encompasses endurance, perseverance, and steadfastness. The Quran frequently emphasises the importance of patience, especially in times of hardship:

> "O you who have believed, seek help through patience and prayer. Indeed, Allah is with the patient." - Quran (2:153)

This verse highlights the dual approach of combining patience with prayer to seek Allah's help and guidance. Patience is not merely passive waiting but an active state of enduring difficulties with a firm trust in Allah's wisdom and timing.

The Prophet Muhammad (peace be upon him) exemplified patience in numerous instances. One such example is his reaction to the severe persecution he and his followers faced in Mecca. Despite the intense pressure, he remained steadfast, never losing hope or resorting to anger. His patience was rooted in his deep trust in Allah and his understanding that trials are part of the divine plan.

In another instance, during the Year of Sorrow, when he lost his beloved wife Khadijah and his uncle Abu Talib, the Prophet (peace be upon him) exhibited immense patience. He continued his mission with determination, knowing that his strength lay in his unwavering faith.

Prayer (Salah) as a Source of Strength and Comfort

Prayer (Salah) is a cornerstone of Islamic worship and a powerful tool for coping with stress and adversity. The act of praying provides a direct connection to Allah, offering spiritual solace and mental peace. The Quran underscores the importance of prayer in seeking assistance:

> *"And seek help through patience and prayer, and indeed, it is difficult except for the humbly submissive [to Allah]."*
> *- Quran (2:45)*

This verse illustrates that prayer, combined with patience, is a profound source of help for believers. It emphasises that true solace is found in turning to Allah with humility and sincerity.

The Prophet Muhammad (peace be upon him) consistently turned to prayer in times of difficulty. For instance, during the Battle of Badr, when the Muslim army was vastly outnumbered, the Prophet (peace be upon him) spent the night in prayer, seeking Allah's assistance and protection. His reliance on prayer exemplified his deep trust in Allah and highlighted prayer as a means of finding strength and guidance.

In personal moments of distress, the Prophet (peace be upon him) would also turn to prayer. A notable example is the night of the Isra and Mi'raj, a miraculous journey that occurred during a particularly challenging period in his life. During this journey, Allah bestowed upon the Prophet (peace be upon him) the five daily prayers, signifying the importance of Salah as a refuge and a source of comfort for the believers.

Integrating Patience and Prayer in Daily Life

To emulate the Prophet's (peace be upon him) methods of coping with stress, it is essential to integrate patience and prayer into our daily lives. Here are practical steps to achieve this:

Developing Patience (Sabr)

- **Understanding Trials as Tests**: Recognise that hardships are tests from Allah meant to strengthen our faith. The Quran states:

    "And We will surely test you with something of fear and hunger and a loss of wealth and lives and fruits, but give good tidings to the patient" (Quran 2:155)

Understanding this can help reframe challenges as opportunities for spiritual growth.

- **Mindfulness and Reflection**: Practice mindfulness and reflection to cultivate patience. Reflect on the Prophet's (peace be upon him) life and how he handled adversity with grace. Regularly remind yourself of the temporary nature of trials and the eternal reward for patience.

- **Gratitude**: Cultivate a habit of gratitude. By focu on the blessings we have, we can develop a more positive outlook, which in turn fosters patience. The Prophet (peace be upon him) said:

"How wonderful is the affair of the believer, for his affairs are all good, and this applies to no one but the believer. If something good happens to him, he is thankful, and that is good for him. If something bad happens to him, he bears it with patience, and that is good for him" (Sahih Muslim)

Incorporating Prayer (Salah)

- **Prioritising Prayer**: Make prayer a non-negotiable part of your daily routine. Schedule your day around the five daily prayers, ensuring that you give each prayer its due importance and perform it with full concentration and humility.

- **Seeking Solace in Prayer**: Use prayer as a moment to disconnect from worldly stresses and reconnect with Allah. Approach each prayer as an opportunity to seek guidance, strength, and comfort from Allah. Remember the words of the Prophet (peace be upon him) who said:

- **Additional Prayers and Supplications**: In times of stress, engage in additional prayers (Nafl) and supplications (Dua). The night prayer (Tahajjud) is particularly powerful for seeking Allah's help and finding peace. The Prophet (peace be upon him) said:

"The best prayer after the obligatory prayers is the night prayer" (Sahih Muslim)

Developing Emotional Resilience Through Faith-Based Practices

In Islam, developing emotional resilience is deeply intertwined with faith-based practices that provide spiritual strength, guidance, and a sense of purpose.

Trusting in Allah's Plan (Tawakkul)

One of the fundamental aspects of emotional resilience in Islam is Tawakkul, which means placing complete trust in Allah. This trust is not passive reliance but an active engagement with life's challenges while firmly believing that Allah's wisdom surpasses our understanding. The Quran reassures us:

> *"And whoever fears Allah – He will make for him a way out. And will provide for him from where he does not expect. And whoever relies upon Allah – then He is sufficient for him." - Quran (65:2-3)*

When you face adversity, remind yourself that Allah is in control. This belief can significantly reduce anxiety and stress, providing a stable emotional foundation. By trusting in Allah's plan, you can let go of excessive worry and focus on constructive actions.

Practicing Gratitude (Shukr)

Gratitude, or Shukr, is another powerful practice that fosters emotional resilience. By recognising and appreciating the blessings in your life, you can shift your focus from what's lacking to what's abundant. The Quran emphasises the importance of gratitude:

> *"If you are grateful, I will surely increase you [in favor]; but if you deny, indeed, My punishment is severe."* - Quran (14:7)

Gratitude helps you maintain a positive outlook even during tough times. Make it a habit to regularly count your blessings, no matter how small. This practice can uplift your spirits and reinforce your resilience.

Regular Prayer (Salah) and Supplication (Dua)

Regular prayer (Salah) and supplication (Dua) are central to Islamic practice and are vital for emotional resilience. Salah provides structure to your day, creating moments of peace and reflection. It serves as a reminder of your connection to Allah and your higher purpose. The Prophet Muhammad (peace be upon him) found comfort in prayer, as he said:

> *"The coolness of my eyes is in prayer." (Sunan An-Nasa'i)*

In addition to Salah, making Dua allows you to express your concerns and seek Allah's help directly. This personal communication with Allah can be incredibly comforting and empowering. When you face emotional turmoil, turn to Dua, asking Allah for strength, guidance, and patience.

Embracing Patience (Sabr)

Patience, or Sabr, is a cornerstone of Islamic resilience. It involves enduring difficulties with a calm and steadfast heart, trusting that Allah will reward your patience. The Quran beautifully emphasises the importance of patience:

> "And We will surely test you with something of fear and hunger and a loss of wealth and lives and fruits, but give good tidings to the patient." (Quran 2:155)

When you encounter challenges, practice patience by reminding yourself of the temporary nature of this world and the eternal rewards promised by Allah. This perspective can help you stay composed and focused, even in the face of adversity.

Engaging in Dhikr (Remembrance of Allah)

Dhikr, the remembrance of Allah, is a powerful practice for maintaining emotional resilience. By regularly engaging in Dhikr, you can keep your heart and mind focused on Allah, reducing feelings of stress and anxiety. The Quran offers a beautiful reminder:

> "Men who remember Allah while standing or sitting or lying on their sides and contemplate the creation of the heavens and the earth, [saying], "Our Lord, You have not created this in vain. Exalted are You! Please protect us from the punishment of the Hellfire." (Quran 3:191)

This verse highlights how Dhikr can encompass not just specific phrases but also contemplation of Allah's creation. By reflecting on the wonders of the universe, we are naturally drawn to remember the Creator. These moments of remembrance, however simple, can bring a sense of peace and perspective during challenging times.

Consider incorporating Dhikr into your routine, even for a few minutes each day. You might be surprised by the sense of calm and grounding it brings.

Incorporate Dhikr into your daily routine by reciting phrases like "SubhanAllah" (Glory be to Allah), "Alhamdulillah" (All praise is due to Allah), and "Allahu Akbar" (Allah is the Greatest). These simple yet profound phrases can provide immense comfort and help you stay resilient.

Reflecting on the Lives of Prophets and Companions

Reflecting on the lives of the Prophets and the companions of the Prophet Muhammad (peace be upon him) can offer valuable lessons in resilience. Their stories are filled with examples of perseverance, faith, and unwavering trust in Allah. For instance, Prophet Ayyub (Job) is renowned for his patience and resilience in the face of immense suffering. Reflecting on his story can inspire you to remain steadfast during your own trials.

Seeking Support from the Community

Islam places great emphasis on the importance of community and mutual support. Engaging with your community, whether through family, friends, or local Islamic centres, can provide emotional support and practical help. The Prophet Muhammad (peace be upon him) said:

> *"The believers, in their mutual kindness, compassion, and sympathy, are just like one body. When one of the limbs suffers, the whole body responds to it with wakefulness and fever." (Sahih Bukhari)*

Reach out to your community during times of stress. Sharing your struggles and receiving support can significantly enhance your emotional resilience.

Maintaining a Balanced Life

Islam encourages maintaining a balance between different aspects of life, including worship, work, and leisure. Ensuring that you have time for relaxation and activities you enjoy can help you manage stress and stay resilient.

Take care of your physical health through regular exercise, healthy eating, and adequate rest. Engaging in hobbies and spending time with loved ones can also contribute to a balanced and resilient life.

Techniques for Stress Reduction and Relaxation

Incorporating Mindfulness and Relaxation Techniques (Dhikr and Meditation)

Dhikr, or the remembrance of Allah, is a fundamental practice in Islam that involves reciting specific phrases or supplications that praise and glorify Allah. It serves as a powerful tool for calming the mind, reducing stress, and nurturing a sense of spiritual tranquillity.

The Quran emphasises the significance of Dhikr:

> *"Verily, in the remembrance of Allah do hearts find rest."*
> *- Quran (13:28)*

Engaging in Dhikr helps to anchor the mind and soul, diverting attention from worldly anxieties and reconnecting with the divine. By regularly incorporating Dhikr into your daily routine, you can create a sanctuary of peace within yourself, regardless of external circumstances.

Practical Dhikr Practices for Stress Relief

Morning and Evening Adhkar: The Prophet Muhammad (peace be upon him) taught specific supplications and phrases to be recited in the morning and evening. These Adhkar serve as spiritual armour, protecting you from stress and anxiety throughout the day.

For example, reciting "SubhanAllah" (Glory be to Allah), "Alhamdulillah" (All praise is due to Allah), and "Allahu Akbar" (Allah is the Greatest) 33 times each after every Salah can foster a deep sense of peace and gratitude.

Istighfar (Seeking Forgiveness): Regularly seeking Allah's forgiveness by saying "Astaghfirullah" (I seek forgiveness from Allah) can alleviate the burden of guilt and stress. The Prophet (peace be upon him) said:

> *"Whoever says, 'Astaghfirullah wa atubu ilayh (I seek forgiveness from Allah and repent to Him)' 100 times a day, his sins will be forgiven even if they are as much as the foam of the sea" (Sahih Muslim)*

This practice not only purifies the soul but also brings immense relief from anxiety.

Tasbih (Prayer Beads): Using prayer beads to count repetitions of Dhikr can enhance concentration and mindfulness. The tactile experience of moving each bead provides a physical anchor that helps maintain focus and reduces mental clutter.

Islamic Meditation: Focusing the Mind and Heart

Meditation in Islam involves focused contemplation and mindfulness, aiming to deepen one's spiritual connection and achieve inner peace.

While traditional meditation techniques often emphasise emptying the mind, Islamic meditation focuses on filling the heart and mind with the remembrance of Allah and reflection on His attributes.

Practical Islamic Meditation Techniques

Muraqabah (Meditative Vigilance): Muraqabah involves deep contemplation and awareness of Allah's presence. Find a quiet place, sit comfortably, and close your eyes. Begin by reciting "Bismillah" (In the name of Allah) and focus on your breathing.

As you breathe in and out, silently repeat phrases like "Ya Allah" or "La ilaha illallah" (There is no god but Allah). This practice helps centre your thoughts on Allah and cultivates a profound sense of peace and presence.

Tafakkur (Reflective Meditation): Engage in Tafakkur by reflecting on the signs of Allah in the universe. The Quran encourages this practice:

> *"Indeed, in the creation of the heavens and the earth and the alternation of the night and the day are signs for those of understanding." - Quran (3:190)*

Spend time in nature, observing the beauty and complexity of creation, and contemplate Allah's greatness and wisdom. This reflective meditation fosters gratitude and reduces stress by shifting focus from personal worries to the magnificence of Allah's creation.

Visualisation of Quranic Scenes: Visualise scenes from the Quran that bring peace and tranquillity. For instance, imagine the serene gardens and rivers described in Jannah (Paradise). The Quran describes these scenes vividly:

> *"But those who have believed and done righteous deeds - they will have gardens beneath which rivers flow. That is the great attainment."* - Quran (85:11)

Visualising these scenes can transport your mind to a place of spiritual comfort and reduce stress.

Combining Dhikr and Meditation

Combining Dhikr with meditation can amplify the benefits of both practices, creating a comprehensive approach to stress reduction and relaxation. Here's a step-by-step guide to integrating these practices:

1. **Choose a Quiet Space**: Find a peaceful environment free from distractions. Sit comfortably, close your eyes, and take a few deep breaths to settle your mind.

2. **Begin with Dhikr**: Start by reciting phrases of Dhikr, such as "SubhanAllah," "Alhamdulillah," and "Allahu Akbar." Repeat these phrases slowly and mindfully, focusing on their meanings and allowing each word to resonate in your heart.

3. **Transition to Meditation**: After a few minutes of Dhikr, transition into meditation. Focus on your breathing, and as you inhale and exhale, silently recite a chosen phrase like "Ya Allah." Maintain this focus for several minutes, letting the repetition of Allah's name calm your mind and soul.

4. **Reflect and Contemplate**: Conclude your session with a period of Tafakkur. Reflect on Allah's blessings in your life and the signs of His presence around you. Allow these reflections to deepen your sense of gratitude and connection to Allah.

Incorporating Dhikr and meditation into your daily routine offers a profound way to manage stress and cultivate inner peace. These practices not only provide immediate relief from anxiety but also strengthen your spiritual resilience, enabling you to navigate life's challenges with a calm and composed heart.

Engaging in physical activities and hobbies to relieve stress

Islam places significant importance on maintaining physical health as part of overall well-being. The Quran encourages the care of one's body, recognising it as a gift from Allah that must be preserved and nurtured:

> *"And spend in the way of Allah and do not throw [yourselves] with your [own] hands into destruction [by refraining]. And do good; indeed, Allah loves the doers of good." - Quran (2:195)*

This verse underscores the principle that neglecting our physical health can lead to harm, and by extension, increased stress. Maintaining a healthy body through regular physical activity is seen as a form of gratitude for the blessings Allah has provided.

Prophetic Guidance on Physical Activities

The Prophet Muhammad (peace be upon him) exemplified a balanced lifestyle that included regular physical activity. He engaged in various forms of exercise and encouraged his followers to do the same. Some of the activities he participated in and endorsed include:

Walking and Running: The Prophet (peace be upon him) was known for his habit of walking briskly, which is a simple yet effective form of exercise. Walking and running not only improve physical health but also provide mental clarity and stress relief. The Prophet said:

"Allah will forgive the sins of whoever walks to the mosque for congregational prayer" (Sahih Bukhari)

This highlights both the physical and spiritual benefits of regular walking.

Horse Riding, Archery, and Swimming: The Prophet (peace be upon him) encouraged horse riding, archery, and swimming, recognising their benefits for physical strength and endurance. He said:

"Teach your children swimming, archery, and horse riding" (Sahih Bukhari)

These activities not only keep the body fit but also promote discipline and focus, essential for stress management.

Wrestling: The Prophet (peace be upon him) engaged in wrestling, which was a popular sport at the time. It served as a way to maintain physical fitness and build camaraderie among companions. Physical sports like wrestling can also provide a healthy outlet for stress and aggression.

Benefits of Physical Activities in Stress Relief

Engaging in regular physical activity has numerous benefits for stress relief and overall mental health. Exercise stimulates the production of endorphins, the body's natural mood elevators, which can help reduce stress and promote a sense of well-being.

Additionally, physical activities can serve as a form of mindfulness, allowing individuals to focus on the present moment and forget their worries temporarily.

Practical Tips for Incorporating Physical Activities

1. **Daily Routine Integration**: Make physical activity a part of your daily routine. Whether it's a morning walk, a mid-day jog, or an evening swim, consistency is key. Aim for at least 30 minutes of moderate exercise most days of the week.

2. **Involve Family and Friends**: Engage in physical activities with family and friends to make it more enjoyable and fulfilling. This not only strengthens social bonds but also provides mutual motivation and accountability.

3. **Combine with Spiritual Practices**: Integrate physical activities with spiritual practices. For example, walking to the mosque for prayers or reciting Dhikr while jogging can enhance both your physical and spiritual well-being.

The Role of Hobbies in Stress Management

Hobbies play a crucial role in relieving stress by providing a break from daily routines and allowing individuals to engage in activities they enjoy. The Prophet Muhammad (peace be upon him) engaged in various recreational activities that brought joy and relaxation, setting an example for his followers.

Examples of Hobbies in Islamic Tradition

1. **Gardening**: The Prophet (peace be upon him) often engaged in gardening, which is not only therapeutic but also a form of productive relaxation. Gardening can reduce stress, improve mood, and foster a connection with nature, which is deeply valued in Islam.

2. **Arts and Crafts**: Engaging in creative activities like calligraphy, painting, or crafting can be a great way to relieve stress. The Prophet (peace be upon him) appreciated beauty and en-

couraged creativity, as long as it adhered to Islamic principles.

3. **Reading and Learning**: The Prophet (peace be upon him) encouraged seeking knowledge and learning. Reading books, especially those that enhance your understanding of Islam and the world, can be both relaxing and intellectually stimulating.

Practical Tips for Engaging in Hobbies

1. **Set Aside Time**: Dedicate specific times in your week for hobbies. Treat this time as a valuable appointment with yourself that cannot be missed.

2. **Choose What You Love**: Engage in activities that you genuinely enjoy. Whether it's reading, painting, gardening, or learning a new skill, choose hobbies that make you happy and relaxed.

3. **Balance and Moderation**: Ensure that your hobbies do not interfere with your primary responsibilities. Islam encourages balance and moderation in all aspects of life.

Chapter Eleven

Time Management in Ramadan and Other Special Occasions

Ramadan and other significant Islamic occasions, like Hajj, are special times that offer us unique opportunities for spiritual growth and reflection. But let's be real, they also come with their own set of challenges when it comes to managing our time.

Balancing daily commitments with enhanced religious activities can be tricky, but mastering time management during these special periods is key to maximising productivity and reaping the full spiritual benefits.

Ramadan, the holiest month in the Islamic calendar, is more than just a time for fasting. It's a time for intensified worship, self-reflection, and community engagement. The Quran tells us about the significance of Ramadan, highlighting that it's when the Quran was revealed as a guidance for humanity.

This spiritual weight makes it essential for us to manage our time effectively, balancing increased religious activities with our everyday lives.

Then there's Hajj, the pilgrimage to Mecca, which is another profoundly significant event that requires meticulous planning and time management. The rituals of Hajj are performed over specific days and involve various activities that must be completed in sequence.

Effective time management is crucial to ensure that all rites are performed correctly and within the designated times. This involves not only spiritual preparation but also practical arrangements like having all necessary travel documents, understanding the logistics of the pilgrimage sites, and coordinating with fellow pilgrims.

Preparation for Hajj starts months in advance. It includes getting spiritually ready through increased worship and learning about the Hajj rites, as well as practical preparations like packing and making travel arrangements.

Balancing these preparations with daily commitments can be challenging, but it's essential for a smooth and spiritually enriching experience.

Special Islamic occasions like Eid, Islamic New Year, and other significant dates also call for thoughtful time management. These times are filled with community activities, family gatherings, and additional prayers. Balancing these commitments with daily routines involves careful planning and prioritisation.

Engaging in community activities and spending quality time with family are important aspects of these celebrations, but they shouldn't detract from maintaining your regular worship and responsibilities.

Effective time management during these special occasions ensures that you can fully immerse yourself in the spiritual and communal aspects without feeling overwhelmed.

It helps you strike a balance between heightened religious observance and everyday responsibilities, leading to a more fulfilling and rewarding experience.

Maximising Productivity During Ramadan

Quranic Perspectives on the Significance of Ramadan

Ramadan is a month unlike any other, filled with immense spiritual significance and unique opportunities for growth. As Muslims, it's essential to harness this time to maximise our productivity both in worship and in our daily lives.

The Quran explicitly mentions the importance of Ramadan, highlighting it as the month in which the Quran was revealed:

> *"The month of Ramadan [is that] in which was revealed the Quran, a guidance for the people and clear proofs of guidance and criterion. So whoever sights [the new moon of] the month, let him fast it..." - Quran (2:185)*

This verse establishes Ramadan as a period of spiritual renewal, where the Quran, the ultimate guide for mankind, was revealed. It underscores the dual role of Ramadan: a time for fasting and a time for deep engagement with the Quran.

Fasting as a Means of Taqwa

Fasting during Ramadan is not just about abstaining from food and drink; it is fundamentally about developing Taqwa (consciousness of Allah). The Quran states:

> *"O you who have believed, decreed upon you is fasting as it was decreed upon those before you that you may become righteous" - Quran (2:183)*

This verse highlights that the primary goal of fasting is to cultivate righteousness and self-discipline. By refraining from physical needs and desires, we heighten our spiritual awareness and strengthen our relationship with Allah. This increased consciousness of Allah should permeate all aspects of our lives, enhancing our overall productivity.

The Spiritual Boost of Laylat al-Qadr (The Night of Decree)

One of the highlights of Ramadan is Laylat al-Qadr. Laylat al-Qadr, also known as the Night of Decree or the Night of Power, stands out as one of the most spiritually significant nights in the Islamic calendar. It is the night when the Quran was first revealed to the Prophet Muhammad (peace be upon him) by the Angel Jibril (Gabriel).

The importance of this night is highlighted in the Quran, where it is described as better than a thousand months, emphasising the boundless mercy and blessings it bestows upon those who seek it.

The Quran explicitly mentions Laylat al-Qadr in a dedicated surah, underscoring its unique status and the extraordinary benefits of worship during this night:

> *"Indeed, We sent it [the Quran] down during the Night of Decree. And what can make you know what is the Night of Decree? The Night of Decree is better than a thousand months. The angels and the Spirit descend therein by permission of their Lord for every matter. Peace it is until the emergence of dawn." - Quran (97:1-5)*

This verse establishes several key points. First, Laylat al-Qadr marks the beginning of the revelation of the Quran, a momentous event in Islamic history. Second, worship on this night is more beneficial than worship over a thousand months, approximately 83 years and 4 months. Third, on this night, angels, including Jibril, descend to Earth by Allah's command, bringing peace and blessings. Lastly, the entire night is enveloped in peace until dawn, providing a unique opportunity for spiritual growth and connection.

Laylat al-Qadr is believed to fall within the last ten nights of Ramadan, with a particular emphasis on the odd-numbered nights (21st, 23rd, 25th, 27th, and 29th). The Prophet Muhammad (peace be upon him) advised his followers to seek this blessed night during the last ten nights of Ramadan:

> *"Seek it in the last ten days, on the odd nights." (Sahih Bukhari)*

Given the uncertainty of the exact date, Muslims are encouraged to increase their worship and devotion throughout these ten nights, ensuring they do not miss this extraordinary opportunity.

One of the primary ways to maximise the benefits of Laylat al-Qadr is by intensifying your worship during these last ten nights. This includes more frequent prayers, longer recitations of the Quran, and additional supplications (Dua).

The Prophet (peace be upon him) himself would intensify his worship during these nights, as Aisha (may Allah be pleased with her) reported:

> *"When the last ten nights began, the Prophet would tighten his waist belt and spend the night in worship, and wake his family" (Sahih Bukhari)*

Engaging in Qiyam-ul-Layl, the night prayers, is particularly meritorious during Laylat al-Qadr. The Prophet (peace be upon him) said:

"Whoever stands in prayer during Laylat al-Qadr out of faith and seeking reward, his previous sins will be forgiven" (Sahih Bukhari)

These prayers can include the Taraweeh prayers and additional voluntary prayers, allowing you to immerse yourself in the spiritual atmosphere of the night.

Since Laylat al-Qadr commemorates the revelation of the Quran, it is fitting to engage deeply with the Quran. Recite its verses, reflect on their meanings, and let them guide your actions and thoughts. The Quran is a source of spiritual nourishment, and its recitation on this night is particularly rewarding.

Laylat al-Qadr is also an opportune time to make sincere supplications. Ask Allah for forgiveness, guidance, and all the blessings you seek. Aisha (may Allah be pleased with her) asked the Prophet (peace be upon him) what she should say if she knew which night was Laylat al-Qadr. He advised her to say: "

*Allahumma innaka afuwwun tuhibbul afwa fa'fu anni"
(O Allah, You are the Most Forgiving, and You love forgiveness; so forgive me) (Sunan Ibn Majah)*

Engaging in Dhikr (remembrance of Allah) throughout the night is another powerful way to connect with the divine. Recite phrases such as "SubhanAllah" (Glory be to Allah), "Alhamdulillah" (All praise is due to Allah), "Allahu Akbar" (Allah is the Greatest), and "La ilaha illallah" (There is no god but Allah). These simple yet profound words help keep your heart connected to Allah.

Acts of charity are highly rewarded during Ramadan, and even more so on Laylat al-Qadr. Whether it's giving money, food, or your time to those in need, charitable deeds performed on this night multiply in reward. The Prophet Muhammad (peace be upon him) said,

> *"The example of those who spend their wealth in the way of Allah is like a garden on high ground which is hit by a downpour - so it yields its fruits in double. And [even] if it is not hit by a downpour, then a drizzle [is sufficient]. And Allah, of what you do, is Seeing." (Quran 2:265)*

To fully immerse yourself in the spiritual atmosphere of Laylat al-Qadr, create an environment conducive to worship. Ensure your space is clean and free from distractions.

You might find it helpful to turn off your phone and other electronic devices to maintain focus. Involve your family in the worship activities, as communal worship can strengthen bonds and enhance the spiritual experience.

Practical time management tips for optimising worship and productivity

Let's dive into some actionable steps to make the most of each phase of Ramadan, with special attention to those powerful last ten nights.

Setting Clear Intentions (Niyyah)

Start your Ramadan journey by setting clear and sincere intentions.

This means if you aim to grow spiritually, increase your good deeds, and improve your character, you're already on the right track. Write down your goals for the month, like completing the Quran, praying more, giving in charity, and working on personal improvements.

TIME MASTERY

Planning Your Day Around Salah (Prayers)

The five daily prayers are perfect anchors for your daily schedule. Begin your day with Suhoor (pre-dawn meal) and Fajr prayer. The time before and after Fajr is golden—use it for Quran recitation or quiet reflection. After Fajr, maybe sneak in a quick nap if needed, and then move on to your work or school tasks. Structure the rest of your day around Dhuhr, Asr, Maghrib, and Isha prayers. This helps keep you spiritually grounded and ensures you don't miss out on your primary acts of worship.

Creating a Daily Schedule

A well-planned schedule can make all the difference. Break your day into chunks and assign specific tasks to each period. For instance, morning could be for work or study, afternoon for household chores or errands, and evening for worship and family time. Use planners or digital apps to help keep track of everything. Consistency is key, so try to stick to your schedule as much as possible.

Prioritising Quran Recitation and Reflection

Ramadan is the month of the Quran, so prioritise spending time with this holy book. Set manageable goals, such as reading a certain number of pages or completing a Juz' (section) each day. If reading the entire Quran feels overwhelming, focus on understanding and reflecting on the verses you do read. This can be done in the quiet hours after Fajr or before Iftar. Make these moments sacred and meaningful.

Optimising Suhoor and Iftar

Ensure your Suhoor and Iftar meals are balanced and nutritious. Avoid heavy, greasy foods that can make you feel sluggish. Instead, opt for wholesome foods that give you sustained energy, like fruits, vegetables, whole grains, and lean proteins. Proper nutrition and hydration are crucial for maintaining your energy levels throughout the day.

Limiting Distractions

Identify what eats up your time unnecessarily and cut it down. Social media, TV, and other distractions can wait. Use that time for worship, self-reflection, or beneficial activities like reading Islamic books or listening to lectures. Creating a focused environment will help you stay on track with your goals.

Engaging in Acts of Charity

Charity is a big deal in Ramadan. Plan your charitable activities, whether it's donating money, volunteering, or helping someone in need. These acts bring immense rewards and spiritual fulfilment. The Prophet Muhammad (peace be upon him) said:

> *"The best charity is that given in Ramadan" (Tirmidhi)*

So, go ahead and spread some kindness!

Practicing Self-Reflection and Dua (Supplication)

Set aside time for self-reflection and making Dua, especially during the last ten nights of Ramadan. Reflect on your growth, your relationship with Allah, and your future goals. Make sincere supplications for whatever you need. The Quran encourages us:

> *"And when My servants ask you concerning Me, indeed I am near. I respond to the invocation of the supplicant when he calls upon Me" (Quran 2:186)*

Regular Dua can bring peace and clarity, helping you stay focused on your objectives.

Staying Physically Active

While fasting, don't forget to stay active. Light exercise like walking or stretching can boost your energy and improve your overall well-being. Be mindful not to overdo it, especially if it's hot or you're feeling tired. Listen to your body and find a balance that works for you.

Connecting with the Community

Ramadan is all about community and togetherness. Participate in Taraweeh prayers, join community Iftars, and get involved in other communal activities. The sense of unity and support from your community can enhance your spiritual journey and provide extra motivation.

Ensuring Adequate Rest

Adequate sleep is crucial for maintaining productivity. Adjust your schedule to ensure you get enough rest, especially with late-night prayers and early Suhoor. A good night's sleep will help you stay alert and energetic throughout the day. Consider taking short naps if you need a quick recharge.

Highlighting the Last Ten Nights

The last ten nights of Ramadan are especially significant, with Laylat al-Qadr (the Night of Decree) falling within them. This night is better than a thousand months, so it's a huge opportunity for spiritual gains. Intensify your worship during these nights. Engage in longer prayers, more Quran recitation, and increased Dua. The Prophet (peace be upon him) used to exert himself more in worship during these nights, waking his family to join him.

Make sure to stay up as much as possible during the odd nights (21st, 23rd, 25th, 27th, and 29th), seeking the immense rewards of Laylat al-Qadr. Set aside time for deep reflection, and ask Allah for forgiveness, guidance, and blessings.

Time Management During Hajj and Other Islamic Events

Planning and preparation for Hajj and Umrah

Hajj, one of the five pillars of Islam, is an obligation for every Muslim who is physically and financially able to perform it at least once in their lifetime. It takes place annually in the Islamic month of Dhul-Hijjah.

Umrah, on the other hand, can be performed at any time of the year and, while not obligatory, holds great spiritual significance. Both journeys are meant to bring you closer to Allah and provide an opportunity for spiritual renewal.

Early Preparation is Key

Start your preparation for Hajj or Umrah well in advance. Early planning allows you to manage your time effectively and reduces last-minute stress. Here's how to get started:

Spiritual Preparation:

- **Increase Worship**: Begin by enhancing your daily worship routine. Increase your prayers, Quran recitation, and Dhikr. This spiritual preparation will help you maintain focus and devotion during the pilgrimage.

- **Seek Knowledge**: Learn about the rites of Hajj and Umrah. Understanding the significance of each ritual and the correct way to perform them is crucial. Attend classes, read books, and watch instructional videos to familiarise yourself with the steps and their meanings.

Practical Arrangements:

- **Documentation**: Ensure your passport is valid and apply for the necessary visas well in advance. Gather all required documents, including health certificates and travel insurance.

- **Budgeting**: Plan your budget to cover travel, accommodation, food, and other expenses. Setting aside funds early helps avoid financial stress later on.

- **Health Preparation**: Visit your doctor for a check-up. Get the necessary vaccinations and any prescribed medications. Maintaining good health is essential for a physically demanding pilgrimage.

Creating a Detailed Itinerary

Having a detailed itinerary helps you stay organised and ensures you don't miss any important steps. Here's a sample outline:

Before Departure:

- **Packing**: Make a checklist of all essentials, including Ihram clothing, comfortable shoes, toiletries, and any medications. Pack light but ensure you have everything you need.

- **Travel Arrangements**: Confirm your flight and accommodation bookings. Plan your transportation to and from the airport.

- **Family and Work**: Arrange for any responsibilities at home or work to be managed in your absence. Inform your family and employer about your travel dates and provide them with emergency contact information.

During the Journey:

- **Arrival**: Upon arrival, follow the instructions provided by your travel group or guide. Rest and acclimate to the new environment.

- **Performing Umrah**: If performing Umrah before Hajj, familiarise yourself with the rituals, including Tawaf (circumambulating the Kaaba) and Sa'i (walking between Safa and Marwah).

- **Hajj Days**: Follow the schedule for the days of Hajj, including:

    - **8th Dhul-Hijjah (Day of Tarwiyah)**: Travel to Mina and perform the prayers.

    - **9th Dhul-Hijjah (Day of Arafat)**: Spend the day in Arafat, engaging in supplication and reflection.

    - **10th Dhul-Hijjah (Day of Eid and Stoning of the Jamrat)**: Perform the stoning at Mina, offer the sacrifice, shave or cut hair, and perform Tawaf al-Ifadah.

    - **11th-13th Dhul-Hijjah**: Continue stoning the Jamrat and stay in Mina for the required days.

Tips for Effective Time Management During Hajj and Umrah

Stay Organised: Keep your documents, itinerary, and essentials well-organised. Use a travel pouch or bag for easy access to important items.

Follow Group Instructions: If traveling with a group, adhere to the schedule and instructions provided by the group leader. This ensures a smooth experience and helps you avoid missing any rites.

Manage Physical Energy: Hajj and Umrah can be physically demanding. Stay hydrated, eat balanced meals, and rest when needed. Listen to your body and pace yourself to avoid exhaustion.

TIME MASTERY

Spiritual Focus: Amidst the logistical and physical demands, maintain your spiritual focus. Engage in constant Dhikr, supplication, and reflection. Remember the significance of the journey and the mercy and blessings it brings.

Adapt to Changes: Be prepared for changes in plans or schedules. The large number of pilgrims can sometimes lead to unexpected delays or adjustments. Stay patient and adaptable, focusing on the spiritual purpose of your journey.

Reflecting and Recording Your Experience

Keeping a journal during your pilgrimage can be incredibly rewarding. Write down your thoughts, feelings, and experiences each day. This practice helps you reflect on your spiritual growth and serves as a cherished memory of your journey. Share your experiences with family and friends upon your return, inspiring others to undertake this sacred journey.

Balancing religious observances with daily commitments

The Prophet Muhammad (peace be upon him) led a life of perfect balance. Despite being the leader of the Muslim community and having numerous responsibilities, he never compromised on his worship and devotion to Allah. His daily routine was a harmonious blend of worship, work, and personal interactions, showing us that it's possible to balance religious observances with everyday commitments.

Morning Routine

The Prophet (peace be upon him) started his day early, setting a tone of productivity and spiritual focus. After performing the Fajr prayer, he would engage in Dhikr (remembrance of Allah) and seek knowledge. He said:

"O Allah, bless my nation in their early mornings (i.e., what they do early in the morning)" (Sunan Ibn Majah)

This practice not only set a spiritual tone for the day but also ensured a productive start.

You can follow this example by starting your day with Fajr prayer and dedicating some quiet time to read the Quran, make Dua, or reflect. This will not only nourish your soul but also set a positive and focused tone for the rest of the day.

Work and Worship

Throughout the day, the Prophet (peace be upon him) seamlessly integrated worship into his daily activities. He would take breaks from his work to perform the Dhuhr and Asr prayers on time. This practice underscores the importance of not letting work overshadow your religious duties.

In your daily life, make it a habit to pause for Salah (prayer) no matter how busy you are. Schedule your work around the prayer times instead of trying to fit prayers into your work schedule. This shift in mind-set ensures that worship remains a priority.

Evening Routine

After the day's work, the Prophet (peace be upon him) would engage in personal and family time. He also made it a point to perform Isha and Taraweeh prayers during Ramadan. His evenings were often filled with teaching, guiding his companions, and spending quality time with his family.

You can emulate this by ensuring that your evenings include quality time with family and personal worship. This balance helps strengthen family bonds while maintaining your spiritual routine.

The Companions: Examples of Balance

The companions of the Prophet (peace be upon him) also provide inspiring examples of balancing religious and daily duties. They were traders, farmers, soldiers, and scholars, yet they remained devout in their worship and observance of Islamic duties.

Abu Bakr As-Siddiq (may Allah be pleased with him)

Abu Bakr, the first caliph, was a successful merchant. Despite his significant responsibilities, he was known for his punctuality in prayers and his deep commitment to Islam. He would often distribute his wealth in charity, balancing his business success with his spiritual obligations.

Like Abu Bakr, you can strive to excel in your profession while maintaining your religious duties. Allocate time for charity and community service, ensuring that your success benefits others as well.

Umar ibn Al-Khattab (may Allah be pleased with him)

Umar, the second caliph, was renowned for his strong leadership and justice. He balanced his role as a leader with a rigorous schedule of worship. He was often seen in the mosque, praying and seeking knowledge, even as he managed the affairs of the state.

Take inspiration from Umar by integrating moments of worship and reflection into your daily routine, regardless of how demanding your job might be. Even short breaks for prayer and Dhikr can help maintain this balance.

Practical Tips for Balancing Worship and Daily Life

Establish a Routine

1. **Prioritise Salah**: Make prayer the cornerstone of your daily schedule. Set reminders if necessary and find a quiet space to pray on time, even if you are at work or school.

2. **Morning and Evening Worship**: Begin and end your day with worship. Start with Fajr and end with Isha and additional supplications. This helps you stay spiritually grounded.

3. **Plan for Special Occasions**: During special times like Ramadan or the days leading up to Hajj, plan your schedule to accommodate additional worship and community activities. For example, during Ramadan, make time for Taraweeh prayers and Iftar gatherings.

Optimise Your Work and Personal Time

1. **Structured Breaks**: Use your breaks at work or school for short bursts of worship, like reading a few verses of the Quran or making Dhikr.

2. **Productive Use of Commute**: If you commute, use this time for listening to Islamic lectures, reciting Quranic verses, or engaging in silent Dhikr.

3. **Family Involvement**: Involve your family in worship activities. Pray together, read Islamic books, and discuss what you learn. This strengthens family bonds and keeps everyone spiritually engaged.

Use Technology Wisely

1. **Islamic Apps**: Utilise apps that remind you of prayer times, help with Quran recitation, and track your daily worship goals. These tools can keep you consistent even during busy periods.

2. **Online Learning**: Participate in online Islamic courses or watch lectures that you can fit into your schedule. This can be a flexible way to increase your knowledge and stay motivated.

Reflect and Adjust

1. **Regular Self-Assessment**: Take time to reflect on your routine and make necessary adjustments to ensure worship remains a priority. Seek Allah's guidance through prayer and supplication for maintaining balance.

2. **Setting Realistic Goals**: Especially during busy periods or special occasions, set achievable worship goals. Quality over quantity is key. For instance, during Ramadan, focus on understanding the Quran rather than just completing it.

Chapter Twelve

Continuous Improvement and Self-Reflection

In Islam, the journey toward self-betterment is an on-going process, deeply rooted in the concept of Tazkiyah, or self-purification. Think of it as a spiritual detox—cleansing your heart and mind from negative traits and habits, and cultivating positive ones. It's not a one-time event but a lifelong commitment to becoming better versions of ourselves. This isn't just about spirituality; it's about aligning your daily actions with your long-term goals and values.

Self-reflection plays a crucial role in this process. It's about taking a step back to look at our lives objectively, identifying areas where we are doing well and areas that need improvement. Reflecting on our time management practices, for instance, can reveal whether we are making the best use of our time or if there are distractions and habits we need to change. It's an honest conversation with ourselves, driven by a desire to grow and succeed in both our worldly and spiritual endeavours.

Productive acts are those that bring us closer to our goals while benefiting others. Whether it's volunteering, engaging in community service, or simply being kind and supportive to those around us, these acts nurture a sense of purpose. They remind us that our efforts are not just about personal gain but about contributing to the greater good. This, in turn, enhances our spiritual well-being and keeps us grounded.

Commitment to Lifelong Learning and Personal Development

Embracing the concept of Tazkiyah (self-purification) for spiritual growth

In Islam, Tazkiyah is not a one-time event but a continuous journey. It's like tending to a garden—regularly removing weeds and nurturing plants to ensure they thrive. Similarly, self-purification requires consistent effort to eliminate bad habits and cultivate good ones. Tazkiyah is a recurring theme in the Quran. Allah says:

> *"He has succeeded who purifies it, and he has failed who instils it with corruption" (Quran 91:9-10)*

This verse clearly illustrates that purification of the soul is paramount for success. The concept of Tazkiyah is not a one-time event but an on-going process, much like tending to a garden—regularly removing weeds and nurturing plants to ensure they thrive.

The Prophet Muhammad (peace be upon him) exemplified Tazkiyah in his daily life. He constantly engaged in self-reflection, seeking forgiveness, and striving to improve his character.

He emphasised the importance of self-purification to his followers, reminding them that it is a lifelong commitment. In one Hadith, the Prophet (peace be upon him) said:

> *"Truly, Allah does not look at your outward appearance or your wealth, but He looks at your heart and your deeds" (Sahih Muslim)*

This Hadith highlights the importance of internal purification over external appearances.

So, how do we embrace Tazkiyah in our lives? It starts with a sincere intention. Acknowledge that self-purification is a priority and make a conscious effort to work towards it. Begin by identifying the negative traits and habits that hold you back. It could be anger, jealousy, laziness, or any other vice. Acknowledge these weaknesses and make a commitment to address them.

Self-reflection is a powerful tool in this process. The Quran states:

> *"And those who have believed and whose hearts are assured by the remembrance of Allah. Unquestionably, by the remembrance of Allah hearts are assured" (Quran 13:28)*

Take time each day to reflect on your actions, thoughts, and intentions. Are they aligned with Islamic values? Are there areas where you can improve? This practice helps you stay aware of your progress and identify areas that need more attention.

Another crucial aspect of Tazkiyah is seeking knowledge. Lifelong learning is not just about acquiring information but about gaining wisdom and understanding. The Quran and Hadith are rich sources of guidance for self-purification. Study them regularly to gain insights into how you can improve your character and draw closer to Allah. The Prophet (peace be upon him) said:

> *"Seek knowledge from the cradle to the grave." (Al-Bayhaqi)*

This highlights that the pursuit of knowledge is a key component of personal and spiritual growth.

Surround yourself with positive influences. The Quran advises:

> *"And keep yourself patient [by being] with those who call upon their Lord in the morning and the evening, seeking His countenance. And let not your eyes pass beyond them, desiring adornments of the worldly life" (Quran 18:28)*

Engage with people who inspire you to be better, who remind you of Allah, and who support your journey of self-purification. The company you keep has a significant impact on your behaviour and mind-set, so choose your companions wisely.

Additionally, make Dua (supplication) a regular part of your life. The Prophet (peace be upon him) often made Dua for purification, saying:

> *"O Allah! Purify my heart from hypocrisy, my actions from showing off, my tongue from lying, and my eye from treachery" (Mustadrak Al-Hakim)*

Ask Allah for help in your journey of self-purification. Seek His guidance and support in overcoming your weaknesses and developing your strengths. The power of sincere Dua cannot be overstated.

Be patient and persistent. Tazkiyah is a gradual process, and there will be challenges along the way. The Quran reminds us:

> "So be patient. Indeed, the promise of Allah is truth."
> (Quran 30:60)

Don't be discouraged by setbacks. Instead, view them as opportunities to learn and grow. Keep striving, and remember that every effort you make brings you closer to Allah.

Reflecting on time management practices and seeking improvement

To reflect on our time management practices, we must start by evaluating how we currently spend our days. This involves taking an honest look at our daily routines and identifying areas where we may be wasting time on unproductive activities or distractions.

Keeping a time diary for a week can be a practical approach to this self-assessment. Record how you spend each hour of your day, including work, chores, leisure activities, and worship. At the end of the week, review your diary to see where your time is going.

Once you have a clear picture of your time usage, the next step is to align it with your spiritual goals. Tazkiyah involves purifying the heart and soul, and one way to achieve this is by dedicating time to beneficial and meaningful activities.

Are you allocating enough time for Salah (prayer), Quran recitation, and other acts of worship? Are you investing time in activities that contribute to your personal growth and spiritual development? Reflecting on these questions helps you see where adjustments are needed.

After reflecting on your current practices and identifying areas for improvement, set realistic goals and create a plan. Prioritise your tasks and focus on activities that promote spiritual growth. Break down your goals into manageable steps and allocate specific times for each activity. This structured approach helps you stay organised and ensures that you are dedicating time to your spiritual development.

In the context of Tazkiyah, it's also essential to incorporate regular self-reflection and Dua (supplication) into your routine. The Quran states:

> *"And those who strive for Us - We will surely guide them to Our ways. And indeed, Allah is with the doers of good"* (Quran 29:69)

Regularly asking Allah for guidance and support in managing your time effectively can help you stay focused on your spiritual goals.

Be flexible and adaptable in your approach. Life is unpredictable, and sometimes things don't go as planned. Be prepared to adjust your schedule when necessary, but always keep your priorities in mind. Remember, the goal is not to fill every moment with activity but to use your time wisely and purposefully.

Seeking improvement in time management is an on-going process. Regularly review your progress and make adjustments as needed. Celebrate your successes and learn from your setbacks. By continuously striving to use your time effectively, you can achieve a balanced and fulfilling life that aligns with the principles of Tazkiyah.

Evaluating Progress and Adjusting Strategies

Conducting regular self-assessments and performance reviews

The Quran and Hadith emphasise the importance of self-reflection and accountability. Allah says:

> *"And the Day the wrongdoer will bite on his hands [in regret] he will say, 'Oh, I wish I had taken with the Messenger a way.'" (Quran 25:27)*

This verse encourages believers to constantly evaluate their actions and prepare for the Hereafter. The Prophet Muhammad (peace be upon him) also highlighted the importance of self-assessment. He said:

> *"The wise person is the one who calls himself to account and refrains from doing evil deeds, and does noble deeds to benefit him after death; and the foolish person is the one who follows his own desires and indulges in wishful thinking about Allah" (Tirmidhi)*

This Hadith underscores the value of regularly evaluating our actions and aligning them with our spiritual goals.

To conduct effective self-assessments, establish a regular routine. Regular self-assessment helps maintain focus on your goals and identifies areas for improvement. Start by setting clear, specific goals for your spiritual and personal development. These goals should align with Islamic principles and values. For instance, you might aim to increase your knowledge of the Quran, improve your prayer consistency, or engage more in community service.

Next, take time each day or week to reflect on your actions. Consider how well you have adhered to your goals and identify any deviations. Reflect on your strengths and areas where you can improve. This process helps you stay aware of your progress and maintain a focus on your objectives.

Keeping a journal can be a helpful tool for self-assessment. Documenting your daily activities, thoughts, and reflections allows you to track your progress over time and provides valuable insights into your behaviour and mind-set. Regularly reviewing your journal entries can help you identify patterns and make necessary adjustments.

Additionally, seek Allah's guidance in your journey of self-improvement. Regularly ask Allah for strength, wisdom, and perseverance. The Prophet Muhammad (peace be upon him) frequently made Dua for self-purification, saying:

> *"O Allah! Purify my heart from hypocrisy, my actions from showing off, my tongue from lying, and my eye from treachery" (Mustadrak Al-Hakim)*

Seeking Allah's guidance helps ensure that your efforts are aligned with His will.

Making Adjustments Based on Feedback and Lessons Learned

feedback from others is crucial for growth. While self-assessment is vital, external feedback provides additional insights that you might not see yourself. The Quran advises:

> *"And cooperate in righteousness and piety, but do not cooperate in sin and aggression. And fear Allah; indeed, Allah is severe in penalty" (Quran 5:2)*

This verse encourages us to support each other in our pursuit of righteousness.

To incorporate feedback into your self-improvement journey, seek constructive feedback from trusted friends, family members, or mentors. Their perspectives can provide valuable insights that you might not see yourself. The Prophet Muhammad (peace be upon him) said:

> *"The believer is the mirror of his brother. When he sees a fault in it, he corrects it" (Sunan Abu Dawood)*

This Hadith emphasises the role of constructive feedback in personal development.

Receiving feedback can be challenging, especially when it highlights our shortcomings. However, it's important to be open to constructive criticism and view it as an opportunity for growth.

Evaluate the feedback you receive and consider how it aligns with your goals and values. Reflect on the areas that need improvement and think about practical steps you can take to address them.

Once you have evaluated the feedback, use it to make necessary adjustments to your behaviour and actions. Set new goals or modify existing ones based on the insights you have gained. The Quran encourages continuous improvement:

> *"Indeed, Allah will not change the condition of a people until they change what is in themselves" (Quran 13:11)*

This verse underscores the importance of proactive self-improvement.

Mistakes and setbacks are inevitable in any journey of self-improvement. How we respond to them can make a significant difference in our growth. Islam teaches us to view challenges as opportunities for learning and development. When you make a mistake, acknowledge it without making excuses. Accepting responsibility is the first step toward growth. The Quran states:

> *"And whoever does a wrong or wrongs himself but then seeks forgiveness of Allah will find Allah Forgiving and Merciful" (Quran 4:110)*

This verse reminds us that seeking forgiveness and making amends is crucial.

Reflect on what led to the mistake and what you can learn from it. Consider how you can avoid similar errors in the future. This process helps you develop resilience and a growth mind-set. Make Istighfar (seeking forgiveness) a regular part of your routine. The Prophet Muhammad (peace be upon him) said:

> *"By Allah, I seek forgiveness from Allah and turn to Him in repentance more than seventy times a day" (Sahih Bukhari)*

Seeking Allah's forgiveness helps cleanse the heart and renews our commitment to improvement.

After reflecting and seeking forgiveness, focus on moving forward. Set new goals or adjust your strategies based on what you have learned. Remember that setbacks are part of the journey, and persistence is key. Continuous improvement requires flexibility and a willingness to adapt.

As you progress in your journey, you may encounter new challenges or discover new areas for growth. Adapting your strategies and goals is essential to maintaining momentum.

Keep yourself informed about new knowledge and practices that can aid your self-improvement journey. The Quran encourages seeking knowledge:

> *"And say, 'My Lord, increase me in knowledge'" (Quran 20:114)*

Continuous learning helps you stay updated and motivated. Periodically re-evaluate your goals to ensure they remain relevant and challenging. As you achieve certain milestones, set new ones to keep pushing yourself further.

Acknowledge and celebrate your achievements, no matter how small. Recognising progress boosts your motivation and reinforces positive behaviour. Strive for balance in all aspects of your life. The Quran advises moderation:

> *"Thus, We have made you a just community that you will be witnesses over the people and the Messenger will be a witness over you" (Quran 2:143)*

Balancing your spiritual, personal, and professional goals ensures holistic growth.

Achieving Spiritual Fulfilment Through Productive Endeavours

Balancing worldly achievements with spiritual growth

The life of the Prophet Muhammad (peace be upon him) serves as an exemplary model of balancing worldly and spiritual pursuits. Despite his immense responsibilities as a leader, statesman, and family man, he maintained a deep connection with Allah, never compromising on his acts of worship and spiritual practices. His life teaches us that it is possible to excel in worldly endeavours while staying rooted in our faith.

To achieve this balance, it is essential to integrate our spiritual practices into our daily routines. This starts with making our intentions (Niyyah) clear and sincere.

By setting the right intentions, we can transform ordinary tasks into acts of worship.

For instance, going to work or studying can be seen as fulfilling our responsibility to provide for ourselves and our families, which is an act of worship if done with the right intention. The Quran emphasises hard work and diligence:

"And say, 'Do [as you will], for Allah will see your deeds, and [so will] His Messenger and the believers...'" (Quran 9:105)

When we perform our duties diligently and with integrity, we are fulfilling a key aspect of our faith.

Incorporating regular spiritual practices into our daily schedule helps maintain this balance. The five daily prayers (Salah) are a prime example. They serve as a constant reminder of our purpose and provide moments of spiritual rejuvenation throughout the day. Structuring our day around Salah not only keeps us connected to Allah but also brings a sense of discipline and order to our daily activities.

Additionally, engaging in Dhikr (remembrance of Allah) and Quran recitation can be seamlessly integrated into our routines. These practices help keep our hearts and minds focused on our spiritual goals, even amidst our busy schedules.

Dedicating time to learn and reflect on the Quran enriches our spiritual lives and guides our actions.

Balancing worldly achievements with spiritual growth also involves prioritising acts of charity and community service. Islam places great emphasis on helping others and contributing to the well-being of society. The Prophet (peace be upon him) said:

> *"The best of people are those that bring most benefit to the rest of mankind" (Daraqutni)*

By engaging in charitable acts and community service, we can fulfil our social responsibilities and find spiritual fulfilment.

Furthermore, maintaining a healthy work-life balance is crucial. Overworking can lead to burnout and negatively impact our spiritual and personal lives. Islam encourages moderation in all aspects of life.

Ensuring that we allocate time for rest, family, and personal reflection is essential for maintaining overall well-being.

Setting realistic and achievable goals is another important aspect. Unrealistic expectations can lead to frustration and stress, hindering our spiritual growth. It's important to set both short-term and long-term goals that are aligned with our values and faith. Regularly reviewing and adjusting these goals helps keep us on track and motivated.

Lastly, finding a supportive community can greatly enhance our journey towards balancing worldly achievements with spiritual growth. Surrounding ourselves with like-minded individuals who encourage and support our goals can provide motivation and accountability. The Prophet (peace be upon him) said:

"A person is likely to follow the faith of his friend, so look at whom you befriend" (Abu Dawood)

A supportive community can help us stay focused and committed to our spiritual and personal development.

Nurturing a sense of purpose and contentment through productive acts

The Islamic worldview emphasises that every action a believer undertakes should be imbued with meaning and directed towards a higher purpose.

This philosophical orientation is rooted in the teachings of the Quran and the Hadith, which guide us to align our daily activities with our spiritual goals, fostering a deep sense of purpose and contentment.

The Quran provides profound insights into the purpose of human existence. Allah says:

"Indeed, my prayer, my rites of sacrifice, my living and my dying are for Allah, Lord of the worlds." (Quran 6:162)

This verse emphasises dedicating all aspects of life to worship and service to Allah, fostering a sense of purpose and contentment in our daily actions. However, worship in Islam is not confined to ritual acts alone; it encompasses every aspect of a believer's life.

Every productive act, when performed with the right intention, becomes a form of worship.

The concept of intention (Niyyah) plays a crucial role in transforming mundane activities into acts of worship. The Prophet Muhammad (peace be upon him) said:

> *"Actions are judged by intentions, so each man will have what he intended" (Sahih Bukhari)*

By aligning our intentions with our faith, we can turn everyday tasks into opportunities for spiritual growth. For instance, earning a livelihood, caring for family, and engaging in community service can all be acts of worship if done with the intention of pleasing Allah.

Nurturing a sense of purpose requires understanding that our actions have both immediate and eternal consequences. The Quran frequently reminds us of the transient nature of worldly life and the permanence of the Hereafter. Allah says:

> *"Then did you think that We created you uselessly and that to Us you would not be returned?" (Quran 23:115)*

Philosophically, this balance is achieved through the concept of Tawhid, the oneness of Allah. Tawhid is not just a theological doctrine but a lens through which Muslims view all aspects of life. It implies that all actions should be directed towards the unity and oneness of purpose, seeking Allah's pleasure. This understanding fosters a coherent and integrated approach to life, where spiritual and worldly pursuits are harmonised.

Productive acts, therefore, are not just about efficiency or output but are deeply connected to one's spiritual state. Engaging in productive endeavours with the consciousness of Allah (Taqwa) enhances their value and impact. The Prophet Muhammad (peace be upon him) said:

> *"The best of people are those that bring most benefit to the rest of mankind"* *(Daraqutni)*

This Hadith underscores the importance of contributing to the well-being of others as a means of fulfilling one's purpose.

In practical terms, this means that productive acts should be aligned with ethical and moral values. The Quran and Hadith provide comprehensive guidance on ethical conduct, emphasising honesty, integrity, and justice. By adhering to these values in our daily activities, we nurture a sense of purpose that transcends personal gain and fosters collective well-being.

Contentment (Qana'ah) is another essential aspect of nurturing purpose through productive acts. In a world driven by materialism and constant striving for more, Islam teaches us the value of contentment. The Prophet Muhammad (peace be upon him) said:

> *"Riches does not mean, having a great amount of property, but riches is self-contentment"* *(Sahih Bukhari)*

Contentment is achieved by recognising and appreciating the blessings we have, rather than constantly yearning for what we do not possess.

Philosophically, contentment is tied to the concept of Rizq (provision). Islam teaches that Allah is the provider of all sustenance and that our provision is predetermined. This belief instils a sense of trust and reliance on Allah, reducing anxiety over material pursuits and fostering a sense of peace and contentment. When we engage in productive acts with the understanding that our efforts are part of a larger divine plan, we cultivate a deeper sense of purpose and fulfilment.

Moreover, the Islamic concept of Ihsan (excellence) elevates our productive endeavours. Ihsan means to do everything with excellence and sincerity, striving to achieve the highest standards in our actions. The Prophet Muhammad (peace be upon him) explained Ihsan by saying:

> *"Ihsan is to worship Allah as if you see Him, and if you do not see Him, He certainly sees you." (Sahih Bukhari and Sahih Muslim)*

By striving for excellence in our productive acts, we not only fulfil our responsibilities but also enhance our spiritual growth and satisfaction.

Chapter Thirteen

Barakah and Blessings in Time Management

Picture a life where you can accomplish more with less, where your time is stretched to accommodate both your worldly duties and spiritual aspirations. This isn't a utopian dream but a tangible reality when we understand and seek Barakah in our time and actions.

The Quran and Hadith repeatedly emphasise the significance of Barakah. The Quran reminds us:

> *"And your Lord is the Most Generous Provider." (Quran 68:14)*

This verse highlights that true blessings come from Allah's infinite generosity. By living a life aligned with His will, we open ourselves to receiving Barakah in unexpected ways. By embedding our daily routines with Islamic values, we cultivate a state of grateful receptivity to Allah's blessings, enriching our time and endeavours.

The lives of the Prophets and righteous individuals are filled with examples of Barakah. Take the life of the Prophet Muhammad (peace be upon him). Despite his immense responsibilities as a leader, teacher, and family man, he accomplished more in his time than we can fathom.

His days were filled with worship, community service, and personal interactions, yet he never seemed rushed or overwhelmed. This was the Barakah in his time—a divine blessing that made his efforts abundantly fruitful.

Consider also the story of Prophet Yusuf (Joseph) and the seven years of plenty followed by seven years of famine. His wisdom and righteousness brought Barakah to the land, allowing him to manage resources effectively and sustain a nation through difficult times. These stories teach us that Barakah is not merely about abundance but about divine facilitation and ease in all that we undertake.

As we integrate these teachings into our routines, we find that our efforts are amplified, our time feels more abundant, and our sense of fulfilment deepens. Barakah transforms our approach to time management, making it a source of divine blessings and fulfilment. It's a reminder that when we place our trust in Allah and align our lives with His guidance, our time and efforts are elevated beyond worldly measures.

Understanding the Concept of Barakah (Divine Blessings)

Seeking Barakah in time and productivity through righteous actions

Barakah, or divine blessings, transforms our time and efforts, making them more fruitful and abundant. It is not just a theological idea but a lived reality that can infuse our everyday lives with deeper meaning and fulfilment.

Barakah is the secret ingredient that turns ordinary actions into extraordinary deeds. It's the unseen force that brings a sense of calm and abundance to our lives. The Quran speaks often of Barakah, highlighting its importance and the conditions needed to attain it. Allah says:

> *"And if the people of the towns had believed and feared Allah, We would have opened upon them blessings from the heaven and the earth; but they denied [the messengers], so We seized them for what they were earning"* (Quran 7:96)

This verse reminds us that faith and righteousness unlock divine blessings.

Think of Barakah as a divine touch that makes everything better. It's not about having more but experiencing more with what you have. The life of the Prophet Muhammad (peace be upon him) exemplifies this beautifully.

Despite his immense responsibilities, he always had time for worship, family, and community. His days were full, yet he was never overwhelmed. This is Barakah in action—his time was blessed, making his efforts go further.

To attract Barakah, we start with our intentions (Niyyah). Working, studying, or helping others—when done with the right intention, these actions invite Barakah.

Barakah is also tied to how we conduct ourselves daily. Ethical conduct, honesty, and integrity are not just moral values but pathways to divine blessings. The Prophet (peace be upon him) said:

> *"Whoever starts the day with sincerity, Allah will bless him in his time"* (Sahih Bukhari)

Living with integrity and kindness attracts Barakah into our lives.

The stories of the Prophets are rich with examples of Barakah. Consider Prophet Yusuf (Joseph), whose wisdom and righteousness sustained an entire nation during famine. His actions, guided by divine inspiration, brought about Barakah, turning scarcity into abundance. Similarly, the companions of the Prophet (peace be upon him) experienced Barakah through their deep faith and dedication to good deeds.

Regular worship and remembrance of Allah (Dhikr) are essential for maintaining Barakah. The five daily prayers (Salah) anchor our day, reminding us of our purpose. Engaging in Dhikr and Quran recitation keeps our hearts and minds aligned with our spiritual goals.

The Prophet (peace be upon him) emphasised the importance of these practices, saying:

> *"The best of you are those who learn the Quran and teach it" (Sahih Bukhari)*

These acts of worship invite continuous blessings.

Charity and helping others are powerful ways to attract Barakah. The Prophet (peace be upon him) said:

> *"The best of people are those who are most beneficial to people" (Daraqutni)*

By giving our time, resources, or support to those in need, we invite divine blessings that multiply our efforts. The Quran says:

> *"The example of those who spend their wealth in the way of Allah is like a seed [of grain] that sprouts seven ears; in every ear are a hundred grains. Allah gives manifold increase to whom He wills" (Quran 2:261)*

This verse beautifully illustrates how acts of charity are magnified through Barakah.

In an age fixated on material wealth, Islam offers a tranquil path: to cherish and find solace in what we possess. True wealth is not measured by the abundance of our belongings but by the serenity that contentment bestows upon the soul. Embracing what Allah has provided us with brings a profound peace, redirecting our focus to what is genuinely significant, thereby inviting Barakah into our lives.

Barakah transforms our time and efforts, making them more abundant and fulfilling. It turns our daily actions into worship through sincere intentions and ethical conduct. By seeking Barakah, we find a sense of abundance and contentment that goes beyond material success.

Examples of Barakah in the lives of the Prophets and righteous individuals

Prophet Ibrahim (Abraham)

One of the most compelling examples of Barakah is found in the life of Prophet Ibrahim (peace be upon him). His unwavering faith and submission to Allah's will brought immense blessings, not just to his life but to his progeny as well. Allah says in the Quran:

> *"And We blessed him and Isaac. But among their descendants is the doer of good and the clearly unjust to himself" (Quran 37:113)*

The blessings bestowed upon Ibrahim extended to his children and generations beyond, signifying the enduring nature of Barakah.

Ibrahim's life was marked by trials, including the command to sacrifice his son, Ismail. His willingness to obey Allah, even in such a severe test, resulted in immense blessings. Not only was his son spared, but Ibrahim's faith was solidified, and he was promised that his descendants would be leaders of nations. This narrative illustrates that true Barakah comes from total submission to Allah's will and unwavering faith in His wisdom.

Prophet Yusuf (Joseph)

The story of Prophet Yusuf (peace be upon him) is another profound example of Barakah. Despite being sold into slavery and facing numerous hardships, Yusuf's unwavering faith and integrity brought divine blessings into his life. His story is detailed in Surah Yusuf, where Allah says:

> *"Thus did We establish Joseph in the land to settle therein wherever he willed. We touch with Our mercy whom We will, and We do not allow to be lost the reward of those who do good"* (Quran 12:56)

Yusuf's ability to interpret dreams, his rise to power in Egypt, and his eventual reunion with his family are all manifestations of Barakah. Despite the trials he faced, Yusuf's reliance on Allah and his adherence to righteousness turned every difficulty into an opportunity for growth and success. His story teaches us that steadfast faith and moral integrity attract divine blessings, turning adversity into triumph.

Prophet Musa (Moses)

Prophet Musa (peace be upon him) also experienced Barakah in his life, particularly in his mission to liberate the Children of Israel from Pharaoh's tyranny. Despite the overwhelming odds, Musa's faith in Allah's support brought miraculous assistance. Allah says in the Quran:

> "And We inspired to Moses, 'Throw your staff,' and at once it devoured what they were falsifying. So the truth was established, and abolished was what they were doing" *(Quran 7:117-118)*

Throughout his mission, Musa experienced Barakah in the form of divine support and guidance. From the parting of the Red Sea to the provision of manna and quail in the desert, Musa's reliance on Allah ensured that he and his people received continuous blessings. His life exemplifies how unwavering faith and trust in Allah can bring about extraordinary outcomes and divine support in the face of insurmountable challenges.

Prophet Muhammad (peace be upon him)

The life of the Prophet Muhammad (peace be upon him) is a comprehensive embodiment of Barakah. Despite the immense challenges he faced, his life was filled with divine blessings that extended to his companions and the entire Muslim Ummah. One notable example is the incident of the Battle of Badr, where a small, ill-equipped Muslim army defeated a much larger Quraysh force. Allah says:

> "And already had Allah given you victory at Badr while you were few in number. Then fear Allah; perhaps you will be grateful" *(Quran 3:123)*

The Prophet's life was marked by numerous instances of Barakah. From the miraculous multiplication of food during the Battle of the Trench to the profound impact of his teachings, every aspect of his life radiated divine blessings. His unwavering faith, compassion, and dedication to Allah's message ensured that his actions were always blessed, bringing about profound and lasting change.

Companions of the Prophet

The companions of the Prophet Muhammad (peace be upon him) also experienced Barakah in their lives due to their deep faith and commitment to Islam. One such companion was Abu Bakr As-Siddiq (may Allah be pleased with him), who was known for his immense generosity and support of the Prophet. His contributions to the early Muslim community were always marked by Barakah. When he donated his entire wealth for the cause of Islam, the Prophet (peace be upon him) remarked:

> *"Nothing will ever harm Abu Bakr, after what he has done for the cause of Islam" (Tirmidhi)*

The story of Uthman ibn Affan (may Allah be pleased with him) is another example. His generous donation during the Expedition of Tabuk, when he equipped the Muslim army, was blessed by Allah. The Prophet (peace be upon him) said:

> *"Nothing Uthman does after today will harm him" (Tirmidhi)*

Uthman's wealth, when used for the sake of Allah, attracted immense Barakah, multiplying its impact and bringing blessings to the entire community.

Chapter Fourteen

Achieving Spiritual Fulfilment Through Effective Time Management

Integrating Islamic teachings into daily routines for holistic success

Looking back on our journey, it becomes clear that effective time management, when rooted in Islamic teachings, leads to a life of spiritual fulfilment and holistic success.

The principles of Islam guide us to integrate our faith into every aspect of our daily routines, transforming mundane tasks into acts of worship and inviting divine blessings into our lives.

Time is one of the most precious gifts from Allah, and the Quran frequently reminds us of its value and fleeting nature:

> "Did We not grant you life enough for whoever would remember therein to remember, and the warner had

> *come to you? So taste [the punishment], for there is not for the wrongdoers any helper." (Quran 35:37)*

This verse encapsulates the essence of what it means to live a fulfilling life: faith, righteous actions, and mutual support in truth and patience.

Starting our day with the intention to please Allah transforms our everyday activities into opportunities for worship. When we approach our work, studies, and family responsibilities with the intention of seeking Allah's pleasure, these tasks become pathways to spiritual growth.

Salah (prayer) anchors our day and provides a rhythm that keeps us spiritually centred. The Quran says:

> *"Establish prayer at the decline of the sun until the darkness of the night and [also] the Quran at dawn. Indeed, the recitation of dawn is ever witnessed" (Quran 17:78)*

By prioritising our prayers, we punctuate our day with moments of reflection and connection with Allah, ensuring that our spiritual well-being is always at the forefront.

Engaging in Dhikr (remembrance of Allah) and reciting the Quran enriches our spiritual life and invites Barakah into our daily activities. The Prophet (peace be upon him) compared those who remember Allah to the living and those who do not to the dead, emphasising the importance of keeping our hearts alive with the remembrance of Allah (Sahih Bukhari). These acts of worship help us stay mindful of our spiritual goals amidst our daily responsibilities.

Balancing our worldly responsibilities with our spiritual obligations is key to effective time management. Islam encourages us to strive for excellence in all we do. The Prophet (peace be upon him) said:

> *"Verily, Allah loves that when anyone of you does something, he does it perfectly"* (Al-Bayhaqi)

This Hadith inspires us to pursue our goals with dedication and integrity, knowing that our efforts are pleasing to Allah when done with sincerity.

Incorporating acts of charity and community service into our routines not only benefits others but also brings Barakah into our lives.

> *"Who is it that would loan Allah a goodly loan so He may multiply it for him many times over? And it is Allah who withholds and grants abundance, and to Him you will be returned."* (Quran 2:245)

Acts of charity multiply our rewards and enrich our lives with divine blessings.

Another vital aspect of nurturing Barakah is gratitude. By recognising and expressing thanks for Allah's provision, we shift our focus from what we lack to what we have been generously given. This mindset fosters a deeper sense of spiritual fulfilment. The Prophet (peace be upon him) said:

> *"He who does not thank people is not thankful to Allah"* (Sunan Abi Dawud)

Gratitude transforms our perspective, allowing us to see the abundance in our lives and inviting more blessings from Allah.

Reflecting on the lives of the Prophets and righteous individuals, we see that their success was not measured by material wealth but by their unwavering faith and dedication to Allah's commands. They balanced their worldly duties with their spiritual obligations, inviting Barakah into their lives. The Prophet Muhammad (peace be upon him) perfectly blended worship, leadership, and community service, showing us that it is possible to lead a life filled with purpose and divine blessings.

Integrating Islamic teachings into our daily routines transforms our approach to time management. Every moment becomes an opportunity to earn Allah's pleasure and accumulate rewards for the Hereafter. By starting each day with the intention to serve Allah, structuring our day around Salah, engaging in Dhikr, pursuing excellence in all our endeavours, and practicing contentment, we align our lives with the divine purpose.

Embracing Barakah in time as a source of divine blessings and fulfilment

Our intentions shape our reality. When we begin each day with the intention to seek Allah's pleasure, we transform every task into an act of worship.

This simple yet profound teaching encourages us to approach our daily lives with purpose and mindfulness, inviting Barakah into every moment.

Prayer, or Salah, anchors our day, providing a rhythm that keeps us connected to Allah. It is in these moments of prayer that we find peace and clarity, allowing us to align our actions with our spiritual goals:

> "Indeed, I am Allah. There is no deity except Me, so worship Me and establish prayer for My remembrance."
> (Quran 20:14)

By prioritising our prayers, we invite Barakah into our time, ensuring that our days are filled with divine guidance.

Remembering Allah through Dhikr and Quran recitation keeps our hearts and minds focused on what truly matters. The Prophet (peace be upon him) said:

> *"The comparison of the one who remembers Allah and the one who does not remember Allah is like that of the living and the dead" (Sahih Bukhari)*

This continuous remembrance brings Barakah into our lives, making our actions more meaningful and our time more blessed.

Acts of charity and kindness are powerful ways to attract Barakah. When we give to others, we not only help those in need but also invite Allah's blessings into our own lives.

> *"Believe in Allah and His Messenger and spend out of that in which He has made you successors. For those who have believed among you and spent, there will be a great reward." (Quran 57:7)*

Generosity multiplies our blessings and fills our time with divine purpose.

Embracing Barakah in its truest form demands a profound acceptance of life's divine orchestration. In a world feverishly chasing the mirage of more, Islam gently guides us to a serene acceptance of Allah's decree.

> *"Say, 'Nothing will happen to us except what Allah has decreed for us: He is our Protector.' And in Allah let the believers put their trust." (Quran 9:51)*

By gracefully accepting Allah's provision and reveling in the simplicity of what we possess, we unveil the profound richness of life. This acceptance transforms our existence, inviting an abundance of blessings and a tranquility that transcends the ephemeral allure of material wealth.

Imagine our lives like a bird taking flight, soaring high above the mundane concerns of everyday life. From this vantage point, we see the big picture: a life enriched by faith, guided by purpose, and blessed with Barakah. This is the life we strive for—a life where every moment is an act of worship, every action is infused with divine blessings, and every day brings us closer to Allah.

As we part ways, let's carry these teachings in our hearts. Let's embrace Barakah in our time, making our lives not just productive but profoundly fulfilling. May the Barakah of Allah fill our days with peace, purpose, and a deep sense of contentment.

A Final Dua

"O Allah, I ask You for Barakah in my time, my health, and my wealth. Grant me the ability to use my time wisely and to perform righteous deeds that please You. O Allah, place Barakah in my daily efforts, make them fruitful and blessed, and guide me to always seek Your pleasure in everything I do. Ameen."

Or another beautiful masnoon dua for Barakah:

"Allahumma ikfini bihalalika 'an haramika wa aghnini bifadlika 'amman siwak"

(O Allah, suffice me with what is lawful, keep me away from what is unlawful, and make me content with Your provision, and keep me away from needing others.)

This dua is found in Sunan al-Tirmidhi, Hadith 3563, and is a profound supplication for seeking Allah's help in finding contentment through lawful means and His abundant grace.

Find Out More

Website: www.barakahinbusiness.com

Socials: @barakahinbusiness

If you enjoyed this book, kindly leave a review to help expand our reach so others may benefit also.

www.ingramcontent.com/pod-product-compliance
Lightning Source LLC
Chambersburg PA
CBHW070425010526
44118CB00014B/1902